THE TERMINAL CODE

THE TERMINAL CODE

J.W. Galliger

THE TERMINAL CODE

ISBN

978-1-63676-743-7   *Paperback*

978-1-63730-483-9   *Kindle Ebook*

978-1-63730-484-6   *Digital Ebook*

For my grandmother, Terry.

*Few in my family understood my love for books,
but not you. Like me, you treated novels like bite-
sized candies, often devouring several in the course
of a week, stopping only to examine the wrappers
of those that left an interesting taste behind. You
always encouraged me to follow my dream of being
a writer. I wish I could've shared this finished
book with you in person, though in my heart, I
know I already have. Love, your grandson.*

CONTENTS

AUTHOR'S NOTE

The first time I put on a virtual reality (VR) headset, I was amazed. I was physically standing inside National Geographic's headquarters in downtown DC but my eyes and ears thought I was deep underwater, swimming alongside sea turtles, fish, and dolphins.

In another session, in Nat Geo's VR Theater, forty other staffers and I cringed as a lion in the Okavango Delta appeared to be strutting closer, licking its chops. Later, we meandered down the river as camera crews and conservationists drifted by in canoes. You could look around and see the entire river scene: flies buzzing, distant roars.

Both times, I was struck by the power, sense of place, and the potential this technology could bring to the world. But as we know, the promise of emerging technology isn't always what it seems.

Take social media, for example, built on the vow to bring the world closer together, promoting democracy, freedom of expression, and individuality.

I watched with awe as Facebook and Twitter became central to the rallying cry against oppression during the Arab Spring in the 2010s, only to watch that same technology be hijacked by Russian hackers to spread disinformation and sow discord during the 2016 US Presidential election.

In the United States, Facebook and Twitter have transitioned from being a place to connect to a self-selecting echo chamber. The picture of connecting different viewpoints, cultures, and ideologies has instead become walled (and often wilting) gardens.

As a marketer, I see the same chords being struck by virtual and augmented reality companies. The same songs of disruption, transformation, and connection are all there.

As society becomes more reliant on technology, some may think the "rules" and "order" built into the system can protect us, that our data will be safe, that our lives will be a little less chaotic, more orderly. But as time goes on, we've seen those who create these technologies always have an agenda. Whether it's to deliver ad revenue, sell consumer data, or prop up an industry based on vanity metrics (likes, followers, etc.).

Aldous Huxley once argued, "Technological progress has merely provided us with more efficient means for going backward." High usage of technology has been linked to depression, and social skills are declining. The power of the "real" interaction is diminishing or being lost as new generations are being born and growing.

But what about *virtual* reality?

VR is the closest technology has come to replicating our conscious human experience. It allows for interaction, emotion, and sensation. Could VR truly connect us as a species? Could it bring us closer together, help us share pain, joy, rage, faith, and hope? Is VR the latest balm for our souls, or will it make them hurt more? Or will it go the way of social media and transform from a technological utopia full of hope to a desert of commodification?

I felt compelled to explore this with *The Terminal Code*, a novel that examines the power, potential, and promise of virtual reality through the lens of one man's journey to solve an impossible crime, one that reveals more about the worlds he inhabits and those who live within them. I've always had a deep interest in emerging technology, how it's developed, marketed, used, and how it's effect on society changes over time. Is it absorbed into the zeitgeist, or is it doomed to irrelevancy? Does technology shatter or reinforce existing norms, and can it reset cultural and socio-economic barriers? Or does it deepen them?

This book explores what society might look like if it goes all-in on virtual reality and as it develops as a part of everyday life. Who will be the winners of such a system? Who will try to exploit the status quo? Who will lose? Ultimately, time will tell the answers to all these questions, and this story is my best creative guess.

The Terminal Code is an update to the locked-room mystery that spirals into a much deeper maze, part science-fiction, part thriller. Enjoy your tumble down the rabbit hole into my virtual world.

PART 1

CHAPTER 1

———

Sometimes in life, your mind doesn't believe what your senses are telling you. As Dashiell Kincaid stared down at the body below him, he had that very same feeling.

Looking at the cops around him, he could tell they felt the same. Normally, cops were like a pack of greedy bloodhounds scrabbling over a thick, marrow-filled bone—not wanting to share credit or glory outside their jurisdiction. But even a rabid bloodhound gets scared.

Kincaid had been summoned to a rundown tenement just outside of New Rochelle. A faded yet proud relic of the late 2010s gentrification stood struggling to hold back the crippling tide of entropy that had engulfed the Land of the Free since the birth of SCAPE. SCAPE was the reason he was here. He was, after all, an expert.

Kincaid walked up the stairs to the apartment, pausing just before the bright yellow holographic crime scene tape, and stared down at his wrist. Pale blue numbers flickered across his carpal bones—4:32 p.m. He smiled and, with a gentle thought to the neural inputs in his wrist, set a timer for twenty minutes.

The body of a large, middle-aged adult male lay suspended in a harness. Eight thin wires sprouted from the back of his arms, legs, torso, neck, and head like he was slowly birthing a matte-black spider onto the floor. The only difference being this spider's legs contained thousands of faintly glowing blue nodes. Turned out reality was as solid as nano-thin microsensors.

These trillions of micro-sensors, bio interfaces, and code replaced the real world with the virtual reality of SCAPE. A technicolor utopia where everyone could find their personal Jesus, kill Oz, fuck a harem of women with Dorothy's slippers, become a hero of their own "Choose Your Own Adventure" fantasy world, head-shot legions of players to win the e-Super Bowl and now...die, forever.

A scene tech approached. "Sir?" he said, voice wavering and staring cloudily at Kincaid.

"How long has he been deceased?"

The tech jumped, startled.

Must be new.

"About twenty-four hours, sir. A building maintenance drone found him like this."

Kincaid absently stroked his goatee, gazing at the body below. He reached up just in front of his ear and pressed down. A blue circle appeared. "Snoops, initialize scene scan."

"Snoops?" the tech interrupted him. "Is that the newest AR implant?"

Kincaid sighed. "No, it's my unique personal AR device. It lets me access numerous systems: local law enforcement databases, SCAPE data. Really any kind of surface info on any given person, object, or location. I thought it was pretty nosy, hence the name."

The tech snorted.

What Kincaid didn't tell him was that Snoops capabilities went *far* beyond that.

"Snoops, re-initialize."

Instantly, Kincaid's eyes fogged over, changing the color of the room to a pale blue. The body was outlined in a bright golden yellow. A dialogue box appeared next to it and loaded the corpse's information. "Wendell Huntington. Age forty-five. Caucasian. SCAPE username: TOTHUNTX. No priors reported in the local databases," Kincaid recited. He turned to the tech. "Have you checked how long he was under?"

The tech shook his head.

Kincaid sighed and pulled out two small gray bracelets. He snapped each to his wrist and pressed a tiny button. A sticky substance oozed out, covering his hands before reforming to fit them exactly. The bracelets contained the latest nanite latex, designed to leave absolutely no DNA that could contaminate the scene.

Kincaid gingerly leaned over to the corpse like a conductor in a symphony. He placed his hands directly underneath the main portion of the harness and pressed a small button. A rectangular outline appeared in the metal and slowly slid up, revealing a small screen with four more buttons beneath. He pressed the one closest to him. The screen came to life.

S.C.A.P.E
Simulated Communication Adventure and Personalization Engine
V. 4.5.0
Copyright symbol 2050

Kincaid clicked the next button and brought up another menu. He selected User Settings > Session Info.

"Looks like he started his last session three days ago at 8:00 p.m. and continued until 3:33 a.m. yesterday when it says there was a connection error."

Kincaid turned to the tech and said, "Have you requested the error logs for that time frame?"

"We figured you might be able to help out with that," a thin sharp voice said behind him.

Lt. Captain Victoria Wong stood behind him with an accusatory look on her face. Lt. Cpt Wong was a short but lithe woman. Her slick ebony hair was pulled back into a bun, her narrow eyes hidden behind a pair of glasses. Quick flashes of AR arrays reflected within them.

"Good to see you too, Wong," Kincaid replied. He motioned his hand toward the corpse. "Care to take a look?"

Wong slapped his hand away. She didn't like being touched by men. "Enough with the crap, get to work," she said.

Kincaid smiled. She was right. They needed his access to SCAPE's data logs, which as a security consultant he, and very few others, had access to. The cops could get that information, sure, but the new privacy laws passed at the advent of VR meant it was a bureaucratic nightmare. Cops hated two things: paperwork and time. Kincaid was the answer to both. His stellar track record of successful SCAPE cases in often record time spoke for itself.

"Wong, it's not like you to admit you need help," Kincaid leered.

Wong's hand twitched, and her eyes flickered toward the man and his gaping exit wound. "We've never seen something like this," she whispered.

Kincaid pivoted back to the corpse. Indeed, strange, he mused, but terrifying? Surely not.

After all, strangeness was just simplicity in disguise.

An immersion visor clutched the top portion of the man's face. Dried, rust-colored blood had trickled down from his ears, nose, and mouth, and pooled onto the floor like an oil spill. In the middle of his chest was a large hole that resembled a gunshot wound.

"Looks like a burnt scramble," Kincaid said.

"Burnt scramble?" the tech stuttered, leaning back away from the body.

He eyed Wong, who shrugged.

"Burnt scramble is SCAPE jargon," he explained to the tech. "It's a catch-all for a rig defect that can cause sensory overloads. Think headaches, mild amnesia, and sometimes fried brains. Used to happen way more back in the early days, but as the rig's haptic tech improved, the percentage of victims has gone down, luckily for SCAPE's legal department."

"That's what we thought too, but when our techs examined the circuit board, they were all fine." Wong handed him a small oval disc. "So we looked at the security footage both live and in session... You should take a look."

Kincaid grabbed the oval disc from her hand and raised it toward the body. A green beam of light shot out from the end, pixels dancing like fireflies, until they formed a fuzzy outline of an alive Wendell Huntington, roughly twenty-four hours ago. Kincaid pressed another button on top and a red laser shot out the other end directly at his forehead.

Snoops beeped. His AR fogged and dissolved into the visor view of Wendell's last session in SCAPE.

Wendell's digital Avatar was dressed as a US Army Commando from Desert Storm. Light reflected off a flaming skull with three concentric stars in the middle. The sigil of the Sternschädel gamer's guild. They were one of the most famous E-Sports guilds in the world, specializing in Shooters. Their call phrase "Give 'em Hades" was everywhere on video-game streams, and it even had a casual-wear merchandise line. More of the scene pixelated into focus. Wendell was crouched down below a burned-out 1980 Toyota pickup. In the distance were several broken stone buildings. A light breeze threw dust and smoke from the desert beyond, bringing with it the muffled thud of grenade launchers, the distant screech of fighter jets, and the occasional blood-curdled cry. Next to him were two of Wendell's teammates: a sniper and a medic. The medic was busy wrapping the sniper's bleeding shoulder. His eyes shone with concentration.

"Hurry up with that," Wendell growled. "I don't know why the fuck they put this in here to begin with."

"Put what in?" the tech said.

Kincaid turned. The tech stood just beyond Wendell, pale and looking around at the whole scene like a scared ghost.

"He's referring to the realism movement," Kincaid said. "When SCAPE and other VR platforms came online, traditional shooters like *Call of Duty* abandoned the HP bar for actual blood, gore, and medics. Game designers rationalized that when groups of players fought in war-like settings, they would play longer, hooked on thrill and adrenaline."

They were right, of course, but what they did not anticipate was these conditions allowed players to develop the same chemistry and ruthlessness as a war unit. What once was casual E-Sports quickly turned into a virtual blood sport, with elite units racking up body counts like plates at an all-you-can-eat buffet.

Many casual observers became appalled by the violence. Anti-war sentiments and censorship movements sprang up around the world. As a result, shooters became the domain of only the truly hardcore gamers, and actual former soldiers trying to exorcise their very real PTSD demons with virtual ones.

A grenade burst just behind the tech. He shrieked. Kincaid rolled his eyes and waved him away before returning to his analysis.

"One sec, almost done," the medic replied.

Wendell pulled the walkie from his vest. "Dak, we're all set here, ready to approach from five o'clock."

"Copy, Wendy. We'll provide suppressing fire from Alpha sector. Give 'em a dose of Hades."

Wendell and his two teammates ran across the field, zigzagging toward the building beyond. They got about halfway when the first shot rang out, catching the medic in the shoulder. The force of the shot spun the medic around toward Wendell. A ribbon of blood flew into the air. Pain spread across the medic's face when another bullet flew through his head, splattering brain matter onto Wendell's face, followed by a bright blue pulse as the medic's Avatar de-pixelated out of the session.

"*Jesus*," Wendell cried, grabbing his walkie. "Dak, where the fuck is that suppressing fire?"

Static broke out of the walkie, followed by the sneezing of automatic rounds.

"Wendy, we've got hostiles incoming. Those bastards snuck around us. We can't—"

The walkie cracked and went silent.

"Dammit," Wendell said, turning toward his sniper. Blood seeped through the bandage. He gritted his teeth and grabbed his rifle. "I'm gonna go up to that building to see what I can. You take my gun and cover me, alright?"

The sniper's Avatar shimmered slightly, likely from his own spider harness' bandwidth struggling to simulate the escalating blood loss, before saying, "Copy. Give 'em Hades."

Wendell smiled. "Roger that."

Wendell sprinted away from the sniper. His boots thudded against the sun-cracked earth, bullets whizzed by, their echoes like Greek sirens. The horizon rocked up and down as he sprinted faster. His breath escaped in ragged bursts between the elevated staccato of his heartbeat.

Wendell was about forty yards away from the building when the world lurched right. He flew five feet and landed in a pile of rubble. As he rose, he hacked up blood. He looked down, his chest spreading crimson. He placed a shaky leg on the ground and, using the butt of the rifle, pulled himself up.

Kincaid whistled. Not many gamers could take that kind of hit and get up after, virtual or not.

Wendell stutter-stepped toward the building. Blood fell from his body like the beat of a cruel snare drum.

The edges of the helmet-cam reddened. A sign of low HP. The building loomed above him like a tomb. He had just begun to go inside when a soft whistle blew in the distance, like the gentle twill of a bird. It was the last thing Wendell heard before his world erupted in fire and darkness.

"Snoops, adjust view."

The camera went dark for a moment as it readjusted. Kincaid now stood over Wendell lying prone on the ground amid dust and rubble. Ribbons of blood ran from his eyes, ears, and chest. His pupils were glassy just like the screen of his VR helmet. His Avatar shimmered blue and began to de-pixelate before—

"Pause," Wong said. The scene froze and rippled as the real-life Wong came into frame, outlined in the same pixelated blue. She bent down over Wendell like a Valkyrie. "Look at his injuries, notice anything?"

Kincaid shrugged. "Looks like the cost of a fake war to me."

Wong ignored him. "Look closer. What do you see?"

He bent down toward the corpse.

It couldn't be.

"Snoops, scan Wendell's VR corpse and overlay in real time."

Snoops beeped, and a pale-pink outline of Wendell appeared. Using his hands, Kincaid manipulated the projection to fit directly over Wendell's corpse.

The wounds matched.

Kincaid gulped.

"Snoops, play the security cam footage," Kincaid said.

The green pixels danced, showing an overlay of Wendell suspended within his rig. A cacophony of lights and blue sparkled over his skin, spreading from the rig's spider nodes into his own nervous system.

The major breakthrough for SCAPE was the rig. Without it, SCAPE would still be a gimmick rather than a global force. Early models were rife with feedback errors, burnt scrambles, and even a few deaths. Eventually, limits were put in place to minimize pain and limit other stimuli on base models, though add-ons and other upgrades could increase this, although only to a point.

Kincaid crouched down and tapped on the side of the input, cycling through menus until he came to the rig product info:

Rig Model #011821

Additional Packages:

A-tank (standard)

N-tank (Achilles)

T-tank (standard)

"Looks like he has the latest and greatest rig," Kincaid said, turning to Wong. "No major upgrades other than an Achilles variant N-tank. Which makes sense given his guild. You sure it's not Ritz?"

Wong rolled her eyes. "Wait for it," she said.

The lights on the rig flickered.

A defect, perhaps? It wasn't implausible, Kincaid thought, standing up. All he had to do is take note of the serial number and report it to SCAPE's hardware division. The legal team would take care of the rest. A smooth and easy case.

Then something strange happened. Wendell's body jerked, then the rig turned off.

Kincaid leaned over the digital apparition. He watched in amazement as blood blossomed from Wendell's chest and dripped down from his nose and ears. Just like it had within SCAPE. He was about to end the projection when the machine turned back on.

That didn't look like some hardware glitch.

The rig was *off* when Wendell was shot.

How in the hell could it have overloaded if there was no power?

This didn't make sense. The beauty of SCAPE was for all its surprises, its chaos and randomness was as false as the worlds shown within. It was simply code running in lines across the back-end of a screen. Even the users within the system could only act within defined parameters. Deaths in SCAPE happened all the time, but the user was reloaded to a save point or the game ended.

But this... *this* was a simultaneous death.

That wasn't part of the system. That was impossible, and if true, it shifted this case to something very different indeed, a death done through virtual reality.

A deadly flaw.

He grimaced.

"Victoria." Kincaid rarely used her first name, for that would require mutual respect. "Let me take this one. It looks like I may have to go deeper into the back-end."

Wong nodded.

Kincaid slowly turned and walked out of the building into the city beyond. He had no idea how truly deep he had to go.

CHAPTER 2

Kincaid stood on the edge of the platform staring down at the rusted train tracks below, wondering how quickly he could get into SCAPE's administrative logs. When a breeze picked up, he expected the sad silver silhouette of the MTA lumbering toward him.

Instead, graffiti covered the tracks. Ever since SCAPE came online, taggers and gangs had taken New York City back to the 1970s in graffiti prevalence. The scene across from him was a mixture of guild tags, gang tags, and Banksy-inspired street art. His eyes settled on a bright red scribble that said: *FUXK HIVE!*

He smiled. At least New York had not lost its edge.

HIVE was the latest VR political party crossover to seize the embers of modern society after SCAPE came along. At first, they were a SCAPE-only group, promoting rights for users in the system. But over time, they grew and began promoting collectivist policies designed to make sure every person either in virtual or real life had the necessary tools to survive.

He snorted.

Though Kincaid had to hand it to them. Their branding team was worth every penny. HIVE's logo was everywhere.

On billboards, trashcans, streetlights and even the front of MTA trains.

The-six hexagon shape became more distinct as the MTA finally rolled into the station. The doors pried open like decades-old Tupperware, and he stepped on.

He looked down the car and sighed. Empty.

Those few who did leave their homes took self-driving cars. But he liked the train. Aside from being cheap, the view from the tracks soothed him and helped him think through tough cases.

Rooftop reflections rolled by, and occasionally Kincaid would get a glimpse of a scene: a once-proud brick apartment strangled by ivy, a burnt windowless butcher shop, a lone dog wandering down an alley looking for scraps.

The windows went black as the train entered a tunnel, and he saw them in the reflection.

An auburn-haired woman sat clutching the rail with a tiny five-year old girl perched on her lap. The girl kept tugging on the woman's hair as daughters often do for attention. The woman chided her daughter, who quickly removed her hand and stuck out her bottom lip. As if sensing his gaze, the woman looked up at him, her golden-brown eyes stealing his breath away. She smiled and waved to him, her hand missing its ring finger. The stub was still bleeding.

Taken off guard, he began to turn toward them when the train left the tunnel and in a blinding flash of light, they vanished, replaced by a gleam in the distance.

He clenched his jaw.

As the train rounded a corner, the gleam resolved into the silhouette of six identical hexagon buildings. The glare from the hazy red sun struck the metal-rimmed top of the blue and green glass windows. The Cluster. The head-quarters of New York City HIVE, SCAPE, and all other municipal functions were moved there in the late 2030s in a massive public relations bonanza. The leaders of the day called it progress. Kincaid thought it looked like a spaceship ready to depart Earth, leaving old New York behind. But he did like that his days of crisscrossing town in traffic were over.

His AR contact lens overlay flickered. A blue phone icon appeared at the bottom right of his vision, followed by a chime. He tapped the side of his head. The icon expanded showing *Call From: Dawn—Office.*

With a nod, he accepted the call.

"Hey, Dawn. What's up?"

"Hiya, sugar," Dawn replied in her thick Brooklyn accent. "How was the scene?"

Dawn was Kincaid's secretary. AI had made most administrative office functions obsolete. But AIs sucked when it came to managing clients, and Dawn was a people person.

"Interesting, looks like this might be another long one."

Dawn's earrings jingled over the line, which over time he had learned was her nod.

"You've got a potential client here," she said.

"Can it wait? I was going down to the Cluster to pull some files."

Dawn sighed and said, "She says it's important, *and* it looks like she can pay for my overtime"

"I don't pay you overtime," he growled.

"Well, maybe you should. If I wasn't here being all warm and fuzzy, you'd have no walk-ins at all. Ya know Snoops isn't programmed for charm."

A clock materialized in the upper left of Kincaid's vision, 10:30 a.m. SCAPE's admin offices closed at 5 p.m.

"Fine," he said, "I'm heading back now."

"Great, see you soon, hon."

~~

Kincaid rounded the corner to his ramshackle office in downtown Queens. A slightly faded neon sign framed the metal doorway. *DK CONSULTING CO.*

He placed his thumb over the doorway briefly. It warmed as the fingerprint scanner activated beneath. The lock flashed green, and the door opened. He walked up the narrow stairs.

Dawn looked up from the hover screen over her desk and smiled.

Dawn's hair seemed to have been freeze-dried into a blond '80s perm. Her large, fake lashes framed her warm amber eyes and contrasted with her bright pink lips that were wrapped around a menthol lollipop. Her once slim frame had grown over the years and was stuffed into a '70s floral top that exposed a reasonable amount of cleavage that was accented by a bright gold cross. Dawn came from a devout Catholic family.

She pulled the menthol lollipop out of her mouth with a subtle *pop*. Dawn also was a recovering Juul addict and preferred the candy over the patches, which she said gave her the jitters.

"She's in your office," she said, her eyes shifting to the right. She leaned forward and whispered, "She seems scared, might want to bring some backup." She slid a box of slightly stale chocolates toward him.

Kincaid nodded and walked over to the glass door and peered in. A small dark-haired woman stood staring at the wall behind Kincaid's desk.

The entire wall was covered end-to-end with awards of various shapes and sizes. Below the awards was a long narrow table with even more plaques and trophies yet to be hung, along with a few old books and binders.

The woman stood gazing at it all, amazed.

"Quite a collection, no?" he said.

The woman jumped, knocking one of the binders over. It fell, spilling its contents onto the floor.

She hastily bent down, scrambling to pick up the mess.

"Don't worry about it," he said, bending down to help her pick up some of the papers. "As you can see, I'm not the neatest."

Indeed, the wall was the only part of Kincaid's office that wasn't dirty. Empty candy wrappers, chip bags, and numerous coffee mugs littered the entire room. Remnants of sleepless nights and past cases.

He placed some of the papers in a free corner of his desk and held out his hand. "Dashiell Kincaid."

The woman smiled, flashing her bright-blue neon eyes.

A splicer. As the human genome became more understood, many people began undergoing gene therapy. When SCAPE arrived, a different trend arose. People spliced their own DNA based on their in-game personas.

"Beautiful eyes. They must've been expensive," he said.

She blushed before nodding, her dark curls trickling off her small heart-shaped face and alabaster-white skin. She shook his hand limply before awkwardly retreating to the chair in front of his desk, her hands still clutching some of the papers from the floor. One of them held a crumpled photo. When he noticed which photo, his skin went cold, and he leapt over the table and snatched it from her grasp.

Her neon eyes flew open with shock, and she flung herself from the chair and was halfway to the door, before Kincaid recovered himself.

"I'm so sorry, Miss. I didn't mean to scare you. Please come back."

The woman peered at him reluctantly before slowly walking back toward the desk. Her head tilted toward the photo. He opened his hand slightly, revealing the photo beneath. It was a faded portrait of a woman and a young girl. The same two from the train.

"They're beautiful," she said.

He nodded. "They are. My wife and daughter, Emily and Rose."

"Bit strange for someone with your reputation to have an old analog photograph, Mr. Kincaid."

"Yes, I admit it's a bit uncharacteristic but it's the only thing I have of them."

"What do you mean?" she asked.

"They... have been missing for years."

The woman covered her mouth, her neon eyes resting on Kincaid for a moment. "I'm so sorry, do you have any idea what happened to them."

"Only vague guesses. Unfortunately, I had a major accident right before they disappeared. I don't remember anything from the time."

What he didn't tell her was his memory loss went much deeper than that. Aside from the last ten years, his memory was black and blank. An empty room with no furniture.

"But enough about me. What can I do for you, Miss...?" he said.

"A," she replied.

"A?" he asked.

"Yes. I'd prefer to keep this confidential on multiple fronts."

He nodded. "Absolutely, Miss A. As I am sure Dawn told you, confidentiality is one of our specialties here at DK Consulting. So what seems to be the problem?"

Miss A reached beside her and pulled a manilla file folder from her purse and slid it across the desk.

Kincaid chuckled. "Going old school, eh? You know I primarily work in SCAPE-related matters, right?"

"I know, I didn't want this being plastered all over the internet. My husband was a very private man."

He nodded and opened the folder to find a small photograph paper-clipped to a printout.

Kincaid raised the photo to the light. A shirtless blond man was lying face-up on the floor, his throat slashed, with blood pooled beneath him. Next to the man's head were pieces of a SCAPE visor. His eyes were foggy, his mouth-agape, as if in mid-scream when the blade came to end it all.

"Your husband, I assume?" he said

Miss A's lip trembled, and her neon eyes began to leak tears, which in the light looked like spilled highlighter ink running down her face.

"Yes, my husband Alex, Alex Kyranos."

"The game developer?"

Miss A nodded.

Alex Kyranos was the CEO of Apex Entertainment. A former indie game developer, Alex grew Apex alongside SCAPE to be one of the premier worldwide gaming companies. Rumors had swirled for years the creator of SCAPE, Hiroshi Takahashi, had favored APEX over other companies like Sony, Nintendo, and Microsoft. Each had tried their hand at buying out the fledgling company, poaching staff, and engaging in an all-out PR war to discredit the company's games.

"How did you find the body?" he asked.

"I was in-session with some of my girlfriends playing the new *iSim* game, when I got a PM from Alex saying he was going to be in-game working on a new demo for E3. Normally, that means I'm on my own for dinner. I set my rig to *Sustain* mode and stayed in-session for another four hours. Eventually, my friends logged off, so I did as well. I went by Alex's study and noticed the blue light from the rig shining through the door crack. I assumed he was still working and went to bed. I woke up the next morning and found him like this."

"Do you think they were after the demo?" he asked.

Miss A paused, her lashes fluttering in thought.

"Maybe. Alex did say it was *experimental*. He mentioned it was something he worked on with Takahashi before he passed."

"What do the police think?"

Miss A stared at the wall behind Kincaid, at his awards. He turned, and she appeared interested in his 2048 SCAPE's Security Consultant of the Year Award.

That year, Kincaid had uncovered a virus hidden in virtual pet Avatars that hacked user's security systems to phish for bank account credentials and slowly empty their accounts over the ongoing months and years. Users thought it was an error in SCAPE's base code, but Kincaid had proved otherwise. He was enormously proud of it.

"Miss A?"

She snapped out of her daze, eyes again watering. She turned toward Kincaid and said, "They... they think it was me."

"Not surprising," he said. "Spouses are usually the first suspects in cases like these."

"Yes... I know, but the forensic examiner said time of death likely occurred between two to five o'clock in the morning. I was sound asleep then."

"Do you have a home security system?"

"Yes, one of the highest-end models. Alex was very particular about security as you can imagine. The system showed no sign of forced entry, but the thing is... the video feeds were deleted."

"Deleted? What about the backups?"

"The backups are on an air-gaped hard drive in the home safe. But only Alex knew the code."

"Can the safe company help at all?

"They're trying to, but they say it could take months. Apex's lawyers also say because there's likely proprietary information on the system they'd block any attempts to release the contents."

"So it sounds like you just need to wait for those tapes then?"

"Well, there's more, two things actually."

"Shoot."

"Check the paper below the photo."

Kincaid flipped the photo over. The paper beneath read:

UID#:44054, SID:#20421020A

Log-In: 10:00AM EST

Log-out: 7:30 AM EST +1

"Is this...?"

"Yes, it's a printout from his rig's internal hard drive. As you can see, it shows he was logged in well *after* the coroner estimated time of death. But that's not the only thing..."

"What?"

"Alex and I don't cook. We're working vegans, so we always order in or take Soylent."

"So you're saying…"

Miss A's neon blue eyes flashed. "I don't own any knives."

Kincaid scratched his head. He turned his chair away from Miss A slightly, musing. "Hmm… so you're saying you've been accused of murdering your husband with a knife you don't own while sleeping? How daring of you, Miss A. I take it the police found that amusing."

Miss A stared at him, her face still. "Turn the page."

Kincaid flipped the page:

[\root:user:akyrio426 073052//20501021

.txt.msg: entr the maze & hark for the terminal code

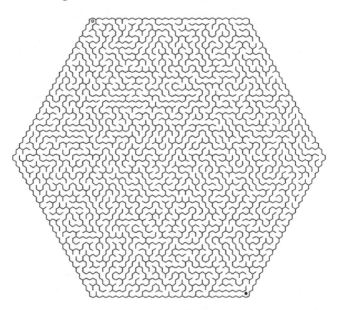

"What is this?" Kincaid asked.

"Before the police came, I found this printed by Alex's desk. I went to check the logs on the rig's hard drive to confirm the data and it kept saying corrupted. I figured you might have the access and expertise to help."

"Have you shown this to the police?" he asked.

Miss A nodded. "Yes… they said they'd look into it. But I could tell they didn't care. My lawyer suggested I contact an independent expert to investigate this. You came highly recommended."

"I'd be happy to take this on for you, Miss A, but I'm actually tied up in another consult at the moment."

Her shoulders slumped, her neon eyes dimming for a second as if she were staring into her own future. She stayed that way for a moment before looking up at Kincaid and pleading, "Mr. Kincaid. Ever since my husband's murder, I've noticed people in suits following me. I haven't been sleeping… I…" She broke into tears.

Kincaid handed her a tissue.

Miss A nodded gratefully, blowing her nose. "I can pay double your rate to take this on, and there's also something else strange I need you to check on."

"What's that?"

"My husband's full Avatar was stolen."

"Full?"

"Yes, after everything had happened, I wanted to log in and—" She sniffled. "I know the Avatar isn't really him but we spent so much time together I thought it would give me comfort just to see it, but when I logged in, it was just an empty gray starter template."

"Miss A, just because your husband's Avatar reverted to the starter template doesn't mean it was stolen."

"What do you mean?"

"After a first time user customizes their Avatar, the Avatar also interfaces with the rig to pull in that user's bio-metric data to create a constantly changing unique customization key. Think of it like encryption on steroids. This provides an additional layer of security for personally sensitive information and helps prevent broad scale account and identity hacking."

She gripped her hands tighter. "That doesn't make sense."

He raised an eyebrow. "The next morning, I logged on this morning to my *iSim* account. I opened the door to my latest house and there his Avatar was, at the kitchen table, sipping coffee. At first, I thought it might be a glitch so I reached out to his bio-data and—"

She fell silent, and tears ran down her cheeks.

"And?"

"He… it.. they... tore the house down, forcing me to log out. But I swear, the bio-data it felt real, it felt like *him.*"

"And his rig, you're sure it was completely intact, nothing was missing?"

She nodded.

He exhaled.

Despite the security features SCAPE Avatars weren't completely impervious. If hackers wanted to steal a user's Avatar, they often had to steal part of the rig and the user's DNA itself. A costly, and often futile process.

Still.

He leaned back in his chair. First, he had a case of possibly the first-ever simultaneous death in SCAPE's history, and now an Avatar supposedly living beyond its user's death with a complete and matching bio-data profile? One major flaw, fine. But two? His gaze wandered out the window, resting on the Cluster glowing like a crown in the midday sun.

His fingers tapped against the wood.

He gazed at Miss A's red, puffy eyes, her chapped lips and worn nails, her furtive glances toward the door.

He sighed. "Alright, I'll take it."

Miss A broke out into a huge smile and jumped across the desk, giving Kincaid a large hug. "Thank you... thank you so much."

He nodded and turned down toward the folder. "Do you mind if I keep these? I'll scan them, of course, but my personal AI is military-grade secure, so you won't see this get out."

Miss A nodded.

"Alright, Dawn will take care of the particulars. I'll be in touch with any updates."

She stood up, thanked him again and walked out.

Kincaid picked up the folder and stared at the labyrinth.

Alex, what's at the center of the maze?

~~~~

CHAPTER 3

Before you entered the Cluster, you could hear it. A slow steady hum that grew louder as the subway escalator rose into the center of the square. Once emerged, you were blinded briefly by the sun before being assaulted by a mass of humanity, drones, robots, and androids swarming around the square and its six skyscrapers like bees surrounding honey. Both alarming and awe-inspiring.

Kincaid hated it every time.

As he stepped off the escalator, he took in the scene.

To his right was the brutalist stone monolith that housed the police force, jails, and military barracks. Security drones flew in lazy arcs to and from hangers above, their red taillights streaking like sparklers. Sunlight caught off the chrome helmets of the few human security force who worked within. Two hundred feet farther right was the tall, sleek, silvery-blue of the Energy and Sanitation building. This was where all the city's waste was recycled and energy created.

The building itself was a marvel of complex engineering. The outer layer was composed of micro-thin solar panels that followed the path of the sun overhead. Just beneath were millions of tiny wind turbines that picked up both the drone traffic and gusts in-between the buildings and just outside. Beyond that, gray water and storm water were collected and recycled through an advanced filtration system, which, in turn, powered an electric turbine.

Directly behind him was the neoclassical Government building. Kincaid thought it looked like someone had stretched the Parthenon sixty stories into the sky before sticking a gawdy brass eagle on top. It housed every branch of the city's government: the courts, city council, and the mayor's office, in addition to other administration offices.

Just after the eagle's wingtips were the first of six glass spires of the Business Guild building. Modeled after the One PPG Place in Pittsburgh, the neo-gothic tower housed the banking, stock market, and major businesses that still needed physical office space.

Past that was the crisscrossing of sleet-gray stone, glass, and green of the Health and Wellness Building. Home to the city's largest vertical garden, urban farming centers, and all its major medical centers. Not to mention, the ever-present screeching and hooting of the building's resident hawks, pigeons, and other wildlife.

Finally, beyond that, was his destination. SCAPE's headquarters. A large rectangular tower of hyper-reflective glass appeared almost invisible aside from the large black cylinder columns at each corner.

The building shimmered. Blue, green, and red pixels darted out of the columns spreading over the entire tower. The pixels slowly merged, and soon, instead of the boring, rectangular skyscraper stood an ancient Japanese castle, its outlines slightly fuzzy—an effect of the massive, augmented reality display engine housed within the columns.

Kincaid smiled.

His favorite part of coming to the Cluster and SCAPE's headquarters, known colloquially as the "Portal," was seeing which building would be projected that day. So far, he had seen the Eiffel Tower, the Tower of Mordor complete with a blazing fiery eye of Sauron, the Taj Mahal, and even Hogwarts. The building was ever-changing, much like SCAPE itself. The schedule of what displayed within the outside and inside of the Portal was a closely held company secret. But that did not stop some New Yorkers from betting on it.

Just beyond the edge of the buildings was his least favorite part of the visit. The stark contrast of the Cluster with the city just beyond. Abandoned buildings, vagrants, and strays roamed the edge as if hoping for some sort of relief to emerge from within.

I see they have become lax with their perimeter.

Normally, HIVE officials patrolled the edges of the Cluster, trying to prevent undesirables from breaking the façade of progress and power held within these six towers. The Cluster, while impressive, was only a futile attempt to stave off the darker parts of human nature. Six giant middle fingers to humanity's evolutionary past.

As he began walking toward the entrance to the Portal, a hush fell over the entire square. Behind him, six large hulking security bots stood by the entrance of the government building, each the size of an ancient Iron Maiden and designed to take damage from bullets, missiles, and grenades. All were painted a deep black with a bright yellow HIVE symbol in the center.

One of the bots moved slightly, revealing the party inside: HIVE's current President and Mayor of the City, Luis Garza.

Garza was of medium build and height, his skin tan, and his black hair extended down his face in thick sideburns. The combination of this, his goatee, and his bright yellow spliced eyes made him look like some predatory jungle cat. Garza was as charismatic as he was mysterious. No one knew his actual age, and his origins and rise to power within the ranks of HIVE was the subject of rampant online debate.

It didn't help that Garza himself would add fuel to rumors, supporting or denying various conspiracy theories on a whim.

Garza and his all-female entourage began moving slowly through the square, the security bots circling like silent sentinels.

Just then, a group of homeless people broke through the perimeter and one man shouted, "Mayor Garza, Mayor Garza, please *uno momento por favor.*"

The bots immediately moved to swarm the man when Garza held out a hand.

"Easy, *compadres,*" the mayor said with a slight South American accent. "If the mayor always had his security swarm his constituents while going for a midday *andar,* there'd be no one left to vote. Right, *señoras?*"

Garza turned to his entourage, who held their hands to their mouths and giggled, then waved the man through.

The man emerged from the bots.

He wore his years in the streets on his face. His leathery, lined skin pockmarked, scratched, and dirty. His clothes were tattered faded relics from a bygone error. One of his gnarled arthritic-looking hands was clasped around an old PCP pipe, while the other wrapped around the wrist of a young boy. His cane slapped the pavement with a dull thwack as he slowly slid forward.

He arced his neck up toward Garza like a supplicant before saying, "Please, sir, *mi sobrino,* he's starving. We've had no luck at the shelters, and the rats have all fled to here." The man gestured to the boy.

The boy appeared to be about eight years old. He wore a tattered orange poncho with an old I ♥ NYC on it. His dirty blond hair was unruly and framed a dirty face, and underneath were blue eyes that looked like they had long lost the childlike wonder toward the world and instead, saw only ugly truths and unkindness.

Garza bent down and put his hand on the boy's head.

"Well, that's no good, no good at all, eh, *nino*?" He pulled the hood slowly from the boy's head before bending down even closer to his eye-level. "Would you like some food and shelter?"

The boy looked up tentatively for a moment before nodding.

Garza smiled. "Excellent choice, *nino*."

Kincaid couldn't help but notice the contrast between Garza's actions and his eyes. His words were warm, but his eyes were cold and empty as if they weren't looking at the boy in front of him at all, but instead through him as if focused on some great task ahead. Something about it deeply disturbed him.

Garza stood and noticed the entire square standing still and staring. He straightened his tie before raising his voice. "This young boy here was starving, desperately trying to survive. HIVE does not believe survival should be a battle. It should be a breeze. That's why, since taking over in this great city, we have worked hard for progress: consolidating the sprawling infrastructure of the entire city here in the Cluster. We've invested in automation, AI, drones, robot technology, food, and medical distribution to ensure every able-bodied citizen both in real-life and in SCAPE has the tools to survive effortlessly and thrive endlessly.

"Because, if you take care of the whole of society, individual happiness, progress, *and* contribution grow as well. Each of these towers surrounding us represent the six pillars of HIVE's philosophy. To thrive together we must secure, sustain, explore, pursue, generate, and govern. Most importantly, we must always be willing to offer a hand to those who reach out. Like this *nino* here. Thank you."

The humans in the square began to murmur, then clap, then rapturously applaud.

Garza looked around, drinking in the energy of the crowd like a vampire.

The little boy pulled at Garza's side. "*Senior?*"

"Yes, *nino?*"

"Can *mi tio* come too?"

Garza looked at the old man, his eyes flowing down to his right twisted leg then back up to his gnarled hands. "I'm sorry, *nino*. The adult shelters are all full. We can put in a request for your *tio* here, but it will take some time."

"Juan," the old man said, staring at the boy, his eyes beginning to tear, "you must take this chance, *si?*" He nodded, waiting for Juan to agree.

Juan looked back at Garza. "Please, I'll do anything. We can share my room and food in the shelter. I can work—"

"I truly am sorry, *nino*."

The boy continued to look up at Garza for a moment, hopeful if he stared hard enough something, *anything* would change his response. When that infinite moment passed, the boy's eyes dimmed and hardened. He lunged into his uncle's jacket and pulled out an old revolver and swung it toward Garza.

The old man reached forward while shouting, "Juan, no—"

A shot rang out.

Kincaid expected ribbons of blood to flutter through the air but instead, the head of one of Garza's female assistants cracked back and yellow fluid and machine parts flying from the cavity in her skull.

The body hit the ground with a hollow thump.

Android entourage, clever. She seemed so lifelike.

The security bots whirled into action. Two surrounded Garza, while the others tasered the old man and Juan. Their screams echoed up the buildings.

Kincaid hurried toward the Portal entrance before the center of the Cluster turned into an even bigger clusterfuck.

~~

CHAPTER 4

———

Entering the Portal was like unwrapping the mystery flavor of a saltwater taffy: you never knew what you were going to get until the flavor assaulted you.

As Kincaid entered the Portal, the smell hit him.

Subtle notes of lilac and rose with an underlying hint of vanilla and almond. The slow babble of a stream, the steady hum of crickets and frogs. A gentle breeze caressed his face, rustling trees and rousing whispers from Kodama and carrying the gentle twill of a Shamisen from a distance.

He appeared to be in the middle of a Japanese garden.

Petals from cherry blossoms danced in the wind. The cherry trees clutched the edge of the bank of the stream, filled with reeds and water lilies. Bright green moss and pink and purple flowers surrounded a small gray stone path that led to a bright red arched footbridge. The path continued to another castle framed by a thick canopy of vibrant cherry and maple trees. Far in the distance was a faint snow-covered mountain that shimmered with golden pink hues.

The sun has just begun to paint its mark on the sky, the bright gold and purples of morning slowly wiping away the violet of night. He could still see the faint twinkle of distant stars and silhouette of the reluctant moon. The entire scene was reflected perfectly by the water below.

Spectacular.

As Kincaid walked up the path toward the castle, he suddenly came across a stone garden with semi-circles drawn in the sand. In the middle of the garden was a burning stick of incense. The smoke curled around a red-framed black and white picture of Hiroshi Takahashi himself. An older picture, Takahashi in his late twenties. His thick black glasses hung slightly off the edge of his nose, his eyes were open and mirthful, and his mouth stretched its fullest grin. In his right hand he held the first prototype SCAPE helmet.

Kincaid guessed this was right before the mass launch of the system. Takahashi, a man proud of his invention, not knowing how it would utterly transform the world. Staring at the photo, the breeze picked up. The whispers of the Kodama grew louder for a moment before stopping.

He turned and found a beautiful geisha behind him. Her white skin shone in the morning sun, highlighting her dark red lips. Her eyes were lined in black and red. Her black hair spun into a large double helix that stretched impossibly above her. And in her hair, a single Sakura flower.

She moved toward him with her pink shimmering kimono, her wooden shoes making no sound. She bent closer toward his face, her eyelash twitching for a moment, pulling up his biodata.

"*Ohayō gozaimasu,* Kincaid-san," she said, bowing. "My name is Yuki. I will be your guide today. What can we help you with?"

He stared at Yuki for a moment, unsure whether she was part of the background or physically present.

Yuki placed her hand on his and smiled, waiting patiently for an answer.

He swallowed. "I'm here to check in on some data logs for some users for a case I'm investigating."

"*Mochiron*, Kincaid-san, follow me."

She led him down the path off to the left and into a bamboo forest that wasn't there before. They exited the forest into another stone garden. A large moss-worn stone Buddha sat in front of a steep stone cliff, its palm outstretched.

She turned back to him and said, "Please present your security credentials," before gesturing to the statue.

Kincaid reached into his jacket and pulled out his ID card, made from the same silvery glass as the building's exterior. As he bent to place the card onto the Buddha's hand, the card transformed into an ancient gold Japanese coin with a hole in the middle. The coin rested there for a moment, shimmering, when a rumble came from above. Water rushed over the edge of the cliff down onto the Buddha. Within seconds, what was once a stone garden had transformed into a waterfall.

Yuki clasped her hands toward the water-covered Buddha and bowed. "Your credentials have been approved."

Always an event.

"As you know, Kincaid-san, all personal AR and AI devices are prohibited within the records hall. Please remove your device and place it on the stone tray. We will promptly return it to you when you exit."

He reached up and pressed down on the side of his head. An audible click emanated, and a small flat disc emerged from the side of his head. His eyes watered, and he held up the disc to wipe away the tears when two tiny pill-shaped dots magnetically latched onto it. These components emitted a soft data beam to an implant deep into his optic nerve, which overlaid AR information on his pupil. The device menu was triggered by eye movement and the sphere was where Snoops, his phone, and all his case files lived.

He placed the disc onto the stone. Yuki bowed once, then she pulled a dark red Shamisen and pick from behind her back. She arced her back and plucked the string once. The note hung over the garden like a spirit as fog began to gather, then thicken. As suddenly as it appeared, it dissipated. A large circular shoji floated next to Yuki. She lifted her hand toward the door, and it cracked open slightly, a pale beam of light reflecting from within.

"This gate will take you to where you need to go, Kincaid-san. If you need anything else, please call for me and I will appear."

Yuki bowed and walked away into the garden, petals following her.

~~

Kincaid walked toward the Shoji, the sides of the door slowly opening. Pale light enveloped him.

When the light faded, he stood in a room. The walls, ceiling, and floor were all a darker version of the building material. Particles swirled and shimmered within them, Kincaid's reflection twisting and turning. There one moment, gone the next.

In the center of the room was a slim glass podium, and in the center of the podium was a tiny metal button. He pressed down; its edges turned green.

After a chime, a female AI voice said, "Please state your area of interest."

The walls flickered, waiting for the command.

"User Records," Kincaid said.

Green lines shot out of the corners and danced in front of his face before resolving first into a vertical rectangle, then eight tinier perpendicular lines appeared. This shape multiplied, then transformed from a 2D to a 3D image. The lines shrunk as if a camera was panning back and soon the image resolved itself into a ghostly green library, each bookshelf containing records of the billions of SCAPE users.

He raised his hand toward the first shelf, the letter "A" appearing just above. He swiped his hand toward the left and shelves began to fly by at rapid speed before showcasing the letter "H." He held up both hands and placed them together in a fist, then pulled them apart, his fingers splaying outward. The H-shelf zoomed in and turned to the side, the rest of the shelves disappearing. Kincaid began walking in place and both the shelf and floor moved as if he was walking in real life. He stopped in front of the file labeled *HUN*.

"Wendell Huntington," he said. The HUN file lit up and a menu appeared. Names began flowing down the screen. There were over five hundred Wendells worldwide.

"Filter Gamer Guild: Sternschädel."

The names slowly faded until only one remained. He reached up and pressed it.

Wendell's profile now filled the screen. His picture flashed between his real-life profile and his gruff soldier Avatar.

Name: Wendell Huntington

Age: 36

Username: TOTHUNTX

Address: <HIDDEN>

Gamer Guild: Sternschädel

Session History

Kincaid reached his pointer finger out toward Session History. The words glowed yellow, indicating his selection. The walls flickered and went blank before a massive timeline stretched across all four. This was the visual representation of Wendell's player session and history. His eye scanned the record, and he could see video clips from past streams, trophies from tournaments, chat logs. All neatly categorized. His eyes moved toward the last dot on the screen.

"Expand."

The dot glowed and the detailed session info filled the screen. Wendell had logged on earlier the previous day; he could see his progress on the map, injury reports in game, and at 3:33 a.m., **EXECUTE: CODE 1D.** Code 1D was SCAPE jargon for a force logout. Typically, these happened during connection errors of some kind.

"Display root logs."

"Please state your passphrase," a robotic female voice said.

Detailed root logs as well as personal information for SCAPE users was two-factor authenticated by a passphrase. The system also listened for distress and other triggers in the voice, along with the biometric data stored on each consultant's security badge to authenticate. SCAPE's system was a bit unique: each user had to repeat their Reality Haiku, a memory device SCAPE devised to help players disconnect after long sessions, helping to prevent the lines between the real and virtual from blurring.

"my reality
dwells beyond this shadow place
eyes shut, now open"

"Passphrase accepted."

The screen changed again, filling with lines of code. His eyes focused on one point.

"Zoom in on line fifty-three."

53:

sys.run_command(1D)/ command_executed .sys. restart sys.launch<pkg_$!>

"Open <pkg_$!>"

The screen changed again, filling with numbers and code. *Interesting. Looks like a rig sensory overload script, but there's... Wait, is that binary?*

"Expand lines ninety through one hundred."

01000110 01101111 01110010 00100000 01110111 01101000
01101111 01101101 00100000 01110100 01101000 01100101
00100000 01100010 01100101 01101100 01101100 00100000
01110100 01101111 01101100 01101100 01110011 00101100
00001010 01001001 01110100 00100000 01110100 01101111
01101100 01101100 01110011 00100000 01100110 01101111
01110010 00100000 01110100 01101000 01100101 01100101
00101110 00001010 01101001 01110100 01110011 00100000
01110011 01101111 01110101 01101110 01100100 01110011
00100000 01101111 01101110 01100011 01100101 00100000
01110110 01101001 01110010 01110100 01110101 01100001
01101100 00001010 01100010 01100101 01100011 01101111
01101101 01100101 01110011 00100000 01111001 01101111
01110101 01110010 00100000 01110010 01100101 01100001
01101100 01101001 01110100 01111001

"Translate into English."

"Translating," the voice said.

The screen changed too.

For whom the bell tolls,

It tolls for thee.

Its sounds once virtual

becomes your reality.

Seek the source from where it sounds

within the maze, beneath the ground.

It can't be—
His hands flew again, moving the shelves to K.
"Filter Username: akyrio426, display root log."
His eyes scanned the screen:

01000110 01101111 01110010 00100000 01110111 01101000
01101111 01101101 00100000 01110100 01101000 01100101
00100000 01100010 01100101 01101100 01101100 00100000
01110100 01101111 01101100 01101100 01110011 00101100
00001010 01001001 01110100 00100000 01110100 01101111
01101100 01101100 01110011 00100000 01100110 01101111
01110010 00100000 01110100 01101000 01100101 01100101
00101110 00001010 01101001 01110100 01110011 00100000
01110011 01101111 01110101 01101110 01100100 01110011 00100000
01101111 01101110 01100011 01100101 00100000 01110110 01101001
01110010 01110100 01110101 01100001 01101100 00001010
01100010 01100101 01100011 01101111 01101101 01100101 01110011
00100000 01111001 01101111 01110101 01110010 00100000
01110010 01100101 01100001 01101100 01101001 01110100 01111001

The entire code had random snippets in bold.
"Zoom out screen 25 percent."

The screen pulled back slowly, revealing the strange maze from before.

Sweat began to drip off Kincaid's brow.

So they are connected, and clearly someone is trying to get a message to someone with access. What kind of message, and to whom? What does this maze mean?

"Yuki."

"*Hai*, Kincaid-san," Yuki's voice said over his shoulder, and as he turned, she bowed as if she had been there the entire time.

"Yuki, could you make a copy of just this error script for me? It looks like something I have seen before. I wanted to compare it with another expert."

Yuki paused for a moment before saying, "*Mochiron*, Kincaid-san. The code snippet will be transferred to your security credential's internal storage. Please keep in mind there will only be three views before the data is deleted."

"Thank you."

She bowed again.

He turned from the console, the walls fading back to normal.

As he exited the shoji, Kincaid noticed the sky had turned from the bright colors of morning to midday. He moved through the garden, oblivious to the man in a black suit following him.

~~~

CHAPTER 5

Chaos still reigned in the Cluster. Swarms of security drones hovered over the square. Bright yellow DO NOT CROSS tape crisscrossed in front of the incident. The yellow of the android's brain still soaked the pavement.

No way I'm getting back via train. Guess I'll have to find a brave Uber in Old Downtown.

Out of the corner of his eye, a woman in a trim dark suit and sunglasses looked at him for a moment, assessing his threat level, before moving her hand, drifting it to just above her left temple, the most common place for AI implants.

He turned toward the edge of the Cluster and the grittiness beyond and began to walk.

In Kincaid's experience, there were moments where logic fled and instinct took over. As he left the pristine and heavily guarded Cluster for the remnants of Old Downtown, his lizard brain stirred, tongue tasting the air. The hairs on his neck raised, his palms sweating, his eyes darting around corners and into shadows.

Old Downtown was a cruel joke. The spiderweb cracks of once stunning glass towers, tumbling brick facades of brownstones, the encroachment of rust, and the herds of stray cats and dogs who roamed the streets picking through meager scraps reflected a cold truth: a city once bustling of life was now dead, all of its promise pissed away through fiber and screens. All that remained were downtrodden outlaws and regretful ghosts. He came to a corner. An old, twisted bus route marker hung over him. Across the street a tattered, bundled, homeless man held his hands over a flaming trash can. He peered at Kincaid, his eyes searching for the telltale bump of a gun or pockets full of wealth. He took in his large frame and decided against it.

PROXIMITY ALERT! flashed angry red in the bottom right of his vision.

"Snoops, pull up radar." In the upper right-hand side, a small square appeared, his current position marked as the white dot in the center. His temple warmed, and a white pulse spread outward. As it moved back toward him, five red dots appeared, surrounding him.

Being a military-grade AI, Snoops had a standard radar and proximity sensor, originally built for stealth missions in military zones but also handy for sniffing out a tail or in this case, tails.

Calculate escape route. He double-tapped the side of his head, switching to mental command inputs.

Calculating, Snoops chimed.

Vivid blue light whizzed past his head, his hair fluttering for a moment. The homeless man across the street clutched his tattered shirt, a dark red stain blooming from his chest as he fell to the street.

The black-suited woman from the square ran toward him, her silver gun smoking.

Calculate faster! Kincaid ran to his left. Another blue flash, and the bus stop sign above him blew apart, its fragments falling like a blizzard.

Two more suited men emerged from behind the alley, one crouching down on one knee with his gun raised from firing, the other behind with his gun raised like an axe. They sprinted toward him.

Escape route calculated.

A map of the street grid overlaid the radar, along with a highlighted blue route line, exactly like a GPS.

In five hundred feet turn right.

Kincaid ran faster, more flashes. The street ruptured into fragments all around him. He turned right.

Call from: Dawn-Office.

Ignore. The phone icon disappeared. A moment later, it appeared again. He sighed. Dawn never called back right away, unless it was important. *Accept.*

"Dawn, this better be good. I'm a little busy at moment."

"Hiya, sugh, I wanted to let you know some blond creep came by the office looking for you a while ago."

"Let me guess," Kincaid said. "He was wearing a dark suit and sunglasses."

"That's *exactly* what he was wearing! How'd you know?"

"Five of his buddies are shooting at me right now!"

"*Hrumph!* Everyone's in a hurry these days, no one wants to book appointments anymore. You need some backup?"

Dawn was an excellent shot and had gotten him out of some sticky situations before, but as another flash flew by and shattered the window in front of him, he second guessed having Dawn here entirely.

"Nah, these fuckers are packing some serious heat. Might need some bigger cavalry. See if you can ping Wong on the DL. I have a feeling this is related to our case somehow."

"Just so you know, I checked the street feed outside the office, and it looks like he has even more friends perched up outside. They look like a pack of puppies who just can't *wait* to see you."

"See if you can distract them for a bit. I'll try to take the long way round."

In one mile turn left.

He checked the radar screen. Three red dots followed closely behind; the other two vanished.

Great. Well, hopefully, I'm fast enough to outrun three of these guys.

Just then, his left arm erupted in fire.

The recoil spun him 360 degrees into a nearby wall the moment after the afterimage flash. His breath left him in a giant whoosh. Gasping for air, he lurched from the wall, running blindly, his vision blurry from the impact, relying only on the constant beeping instructions from Snoops. Every step shot fiery pain up his arm. Its intensity turned the edges of his vision white.

Thuds of exploding sidewalks and searing blue bursts of light flew around him like bees swarming honey.

Eventually, the blurry shapes in his vision-cleared. An unfamiliar alley. A rusted city dumpster. He quickly scrambled up over the edge and dropped down. Tattered trash bags and rat bones did little to break his fall.

He held his breath as the red dots drew closer. They slowly approached before flickering away. He slumped his head against the wall. A dark crimson stain spread from the middle of his bicep to just above his wrist. He shifted, wincing, and pulled back the ripped jacket. Much of his elbow and bicep had been fed to a meat grinder. Dark red rivulets of blood dripped down his arm into the detritus below. Beyond the wound, angry blue and black bruises had already begun to lay claim to what was left.

Snoops, estimate damage.

Green outlined his arm.

Calculating...

Severe muscle and ligament damage to epidermis, right bicep and tricep, multiple bone fractures in elbow and humerus. Estimated blood loss—8 percent. Recommended treatment: Seek immediate medical attention to avoid hypovolemic shock.

What about short-term treatment?

Apply tourniquet.

Grunting, he ripped off his other sleeve and, using his teeth, fashioned a makeshift tourniquet.

Where's the nearest doctor?

Searching...

There are no HIVE-sanctioned doctors nearby; however, there is an unsanctioned practitioner a mile from here. Pulling up route now.

The route flickered into life on his GPS. Right before he was about to hobble out of the dumpster, a red dot came into view. He went still, hoping alone might be enough to dissuade his pursuer. The dot inched nearer. He peered over the edge, the shadow growing even closer.

Fuck it. Kincaid leapt over the rim of the dumpster and sprinted into the street, running right into him. The man startled, fumbled, and dropped his gun. Kincaid grinned. *Snoops, activate Plan Delta.*

Snoops chirped and a loud screech burst from Kincaid's head. The suited man staggered back as if punched in the gut. He shook his head, looking around before spotting something behind him and sprinting away. Kincaid waited a moment before running in the other direction.

Thanks, Snoops.

Snoops was silent. Plan Delta was a last resort. An auditory pulse that scrambled and briefly hacked other's AR overlays, tricking them into seeing whatever he wanted them to. In this case, Kincaid running in the other direction. The effect lasted only for a few minutes and took all of Snoops' processing power. So much so Snoops could only execute it once a day. While it was running, he was on his own.

Huffing, Kincaid rounded the corner to his destination. A faded sign reading *Mr. Qin's Apothecary* dangled from one tarnished chain. The entire storefront was boarded and shuttered. He noticed a small entrance and slammed his non-injured arm against the door like a club as he shouted, "Help!"

The door opened a crack, and thick tobacco smoke flew out, revealing a short, stooped Asian man with a Chinese pipe sticking out of his mouth. He peered at him for a moment, then at the blood on the ground before gesturing over his shoulder and walking back into the store. Kincaid followed him.

Kincaid entered a dimly lit room, full of half-empty shelves, cracked black and white square-tiled floors, broken pill bottles, and an old mahogany clerk desk complete with an ancient manual cash register. Its once shining brass frame was now dull and dead. The man stood behind the desk, watching Kincaid for a moment before softly shaking his head and opening another door.

"Come down," he instructed.

Kincaid hesitated. The man cocked his head. "You want help, or you want to bleed all over my old floor?"

Pain shot up Kincaid's arm, his vision blurring for a moment. He nodded then asked, "Are you Mr. Qin?"

The man inhaled for a moment, his face lit by the pipe's cherry glow, before saying, "Once, I was everything. Now I am nothing. But call me who you'd like." He walked down the stairs, smoke trailing behind.

Kincaid gingerly walked down the wooden narrow stairs into the basement, careful not to bang his arm against the railing. The air grew colder and the room darker. He could barely make out the shape of Mr. Qin in the distance when *flick*, a thin fluorescent bulb buzzed into light, illuminating a dusty plastic sheet hanging from a circular shower curtain rod. Mr. Qin pulled the sheet aside, revealing an old dentist chair, a low cabinet, and a utility sink with some half-used gauze trailing out of it like strands of ancient hair. In the corner, perched on a wooden ledge, was an old box TV.

"Come," Mr. Qin said, gesturing to the chair.

Kincaid sat down, the ancient upholstery squeaking.

Mr. Qin bent down and stared at his wound. "Hmm... very bad, looks like you saw the business end of a Thumper. Very nasty business, Thumpers. You must have some bad enemies. This will take time and stitches." He turned, rummaging through the cabinet before handing Kincaid an old amber bottle.

"Drink. I don't have anesthetic, but that will help numb the pain." Mr. Qin removed the tourniquet and blood-poured from the wound. He grabbed another bottle and dipped a cloth in it before dabbing at the injury.

Kincaid screamed.

"This is only rubbing alcohol to clean the wound. The rest will hurt more. Drink."

Using his thumb, Kincaid screwed off the cap and raised the amber bottle to his lips, sniffing. He recoiled. It smelled like diesel.

"What is this?" he asked.

Mr. Qin looked up and smiled. "Secret family recipe, good for surgery, better for Thursdays."

Sighing, Kincaid drank. His entire throat burned as he swallowed, and subtle notes of cherry wafted up from his tongue. He immediately felt warm and slightly better.

Mr. Qin reached down and pulled off the rest of Kincaid's shirt, causing a pin to fall onto Kincaid's lap.

What the hell is this? Kincaid held it to the light. The pin was small, golden, and circular, engraved in the middle was three letters, two N's sandwiching an A and in the middle of it a small circular question mark.

"Do you know what this means?" Kincaid asked.

Mr. Qin shook his head before turning back to Kincaid's arm.

The pin must have been on the tail he'd run into. The symbol seemed familiar, but... the room spun. The pin dropped out of his hand and rolled out of sight.

"Whoa," Kincaid said, grasping the armrests for balance. Mr. Qin looked up at him. "You lose too much blood. What's your type?"

"B-positive."

"Hmm... might be out of that. Let me test you quickly." He pricked Kincaid's finger with a small silver object. The object beeped, its display lighting up with a result.

"This says you're O-negative."

"O-negative, that can't be right. Try it again."

Mr. Qin laughed. "No, it's correct. The rest of this stuff might be older, but I spend good money on this. I give patient wrong blood packet, poof! There goes side business."

How could that be? I've always been B-positive.

The room spun again, his head pounding, trickling away even more of his now O-negative blood.

"Fine, just get to it, my head hurts."

Mr. Qin nodded, pulled the other curtain back, and walked into the darkness beyond.

A red light flashed on and a large gong sound emanated from the ceiling. Mr. Qin's face went white. He darted over to the cabinet, pulled out an ancient remote, and pointed it at the old TV in the corner. The TV miraculously turned on, its screen filled with black and white grainy lines. Mr. Qin grunted, picked up an old can, and threw it at the screen.

The picture shifted before coming in clear, showing a high-angle black and white shot of the street outside the store. The street was silent until three of the suited men walked into the frame. They were staring at something on the ground.

Kincaid's skin went cold. A blood trail.

"Who are they?" Mr. Qin seethed. "Do they work for you? Are you a cop?"

"A cop? No, I'm a P.I."

"A P.I.! " Mr. Qin ran into the darkness and flicked a switch. The entire basement lit up, blinding Kincaid.

When the light cleared, a needle hovered inches from his neck. Mr. Qin's eyes were wide and blazing. "Who hired you? Frau Lintz! I swear that *biao zi.*"

"What the hell, Mr. Qin! Frau Lintz? I've never..."

Just then, Kincaid saw the rest of the basement. Rows of shelves with cardboard boxes and long tables in front. A large scale lay on one, a massive mound of red powder sat atop.

"Is that *Ritz?* You're a Distro, aren't you?"

The needle pressed deeper into his neck.

Distro was the modern slang for drug dealer. When the streets went virtual, many in SCAPE loved the immersive experience, the replicated sensations. Despite the limits placed in the rig, some people wanted more. That's where Ritz came in. Ritz was a synthetic powder containing a potent mix of pheromones, MDMA, and nano inhibitors designed to interface with SCAPE's body rigs, jacking up the sensory feedback to eleven.

"Who sent you?" Mr. Qin said.

The needle flirted dangerously with his skin. One dose of Ritz was incredibly addictive; users would stay in sessions for hours engaging in bacchanal delights. Despite this, government crackdown was weak. Rumor was SCAPE itself was behind the drug. The perfect way to keep users plugged in and tuned out.

"No one sent me, I promise. I came to *you* running from *them.* Look at my fucking arm if you don't believe me!"

Mr. Qin looked at the screen, staring at the men, their guns, then back at Kincaid's arm. "Fine, I'll treat you but then you go. I don't want *them* knowing about this place."

"If they have scanners, they'll find it sooner or later."

"*Heh.*" Mr. Qin laughed, exhaling more smoke. "You think this pipe is for show? Smoke has special nanobots that interfere with most scanners. Why do you think there are so many fires around this area?"

Kincaid shook his head, amazed. The men at the screen were getting closer. Despite the smoke, he still couldn't take any chances. "I need to use your rig."

"You're crazy! You bring trouble to my door and now you want to use my rig?" Mr. Qin exclaimed.

"Yes, I don't know who those men are or why they're after me. Besides, if they find me, they find you, and I'm sure you don't want that." Kincaid's eyes darted toward the Ritz.

"What makes you think I won't let you bleed out while you're diving?"

Kincaid grabbed Mr. Qin by the collar and pulled him in close. "A man doesn't keep relics of the past for others, only himself. You said it yourself; once you were everything, you had everything: a store, a life, a profession. You wouldn't be patching others up if you didn't still think maybe you had a chance to get it all back."

Mr. Qin went silent before he turned and disappeared. He returned quickly with a needle and sutures.

Kincaid shuddered, his vision swimming.

Mr. Qin hovered over him. "You can't dive like this... the blood loss..."

"I don't have time!" he yelled. "Patch me up while I'm in. I need answers, and I know just who to ask."

~~~

PART 2

CHAPTER 6

It always felt strange in the drop, Kincaid thought.

The vertigo. Bursts of electricity tickling your body. Calibrating sensations. Reaction testing. Faint coppery odors. The strange sensation of being in two places at once. The Abyss didn't help much either.

Logging into SCAPE, every user entered the Abyss, a sapphire chasm of *Matrix*-like code and fractals trickling down into a black hole thousands of feet below. Floating on air, staring down as the system calibrated. Rumor was Hiroshi had a terrible fear of heights and programmed the Abyss as a virtual therapy session.

WELCOME, ARKAIDIA6 text slowly appeared in front of him.

"Hiya, Boss." Floating next to him was a fourteen-year old girl, the picture of sonic and rebellious youth.

Her shiny neon blond hair was tied into pigtails, the tips of which were a glowing blue that matched her eyes, lips, and nails. She wore a neon green *Mystery Machine* logo t-shirt that was torn just above her midriff. Her waist was covered with a dark green and black tartan skirt, latched together with a chrome-studded spike leather belt and knee-length leather platform boots. Topping it all off was a tiny matching tartan beret.

"Hey, Snoops, good to see you," Kincaid offered.

Snoops grinned at him, revealing a sparkling diamond LED tooth grill. R-E-A-D-Y flashed across. She giggled. Many programs, including AIs, had corporeal forms within SCAPE. Most forms were wooden and stiff imitations of real users' Avatars, to prevent confusion. But Snoops being a stealth military grade had the ability to blend in to any SCAPESPACE, however she chose. Including gender, age, and form. The only limit being it had to be a living, moving creature.

"Where we going?" she asked, her head turning.

"Can't you already guess?" he asked.

Snoops pursed her lips. "I have three probabilistic scenarios, but sometimes it's just fun to ask."

He stared at her as she did the same, reading his micro expressions, her mind re-running probabilities in the background.

"Fine, be that way. I'll figure it out eventually. I always do. It's why I'm here. Whatcha gonna wear?" she asked, clapping her hands together. Rows of clothes racks appeared and flew by them. A micro-thin mirror materialized into existence.

Each row contained possibilities and memories. Some fonder than others. Yet these outfits served a dual purpose. While you couldn't hide your bio-data signature from the system, you could obscure it from other users. Depending on the client, discretion might be required, or something a bit louder. This time, Kincaid *wanted* to be recognized.

He smiled. "Let's go with *The Professional.*"

"I knew it!" Snoops exclaimed. "We're going to see *him*, aren't we?"

He nodded.

Snoops jumped into the air, swinging her arms. She practically vibrated with excitement. "Can I locate?"

"Sure, but when you find him, observe *only*. He's bound to have security measures."

"Aye-aye, sir!" Snoops mock-saluted. She burst into a blue light and blasted down the Abyss, blending in perfectly with the other data streams.

Kincaid's body warmed as he stared into the mirror. The Professional now stared back. He was ready.

Then came the worst part.

He fell.

Faster and faster until the darkness surrounded him. Suddenly, it emerged. A sun flare of aquamarine code. The Trinity Node.

Inspired by ancient symbols depicting threes, the triskelion, triquetra, a triple Tomoe, Hiroshi used the node as the representation of the three main zones of SCAPESPACE. They were SOCIAL-SCAPE, GAME-SCAPE, and EDU-SCAPE. *Play. Interact. Learn.* The early tagline for SCAPE ads, back when they didn't own the world's minds.

Each log-in, every user flew down into the Abyss and stared down at the Trinity Node before loading into their destination. Hiroshi claimed the journey helped remove the final roadblock from the sense of dual presence, allowing the user to fully accept and integrate themselves into SCAPE.

The Trinity Node came closer into view. His descent slowed, each node outlined in bright yellow. A soft female voice spoke in his head: *"Please choose your destination."*

Snoops, what's your ETA?

One sec, I think I've... BINGO! Found him. He's in SOC-
SCAPE/MUSIC/PRMARAVE/SCAPEHAUS using his DJ
alias again.

"PRMARAVE/SCAPEHAUS, please," he said.

The SOC-SCAPE Zone outline turned green and flashed white, indicating his selection. He began falling again toward SOC-SCAPE, his speed increasing, the rest of the node stretching into white streaks. Then the world snapped, and he touched down.

Bass shot up his spine.

PRMARAVE, like its named suggested, was an area for dedicated electronic music lovers to virtually rave nonstop, 24-7/365, never needing to break for food, water, or the bathroom. The region was split into genre. Each genre had its own area where sub-genres occupied the same space in a trick of blockchain.

PRMARAVE was housed in a giant fractal lotus. Its shimmering white petals reminded Kincaid of the Portal's walls.

As he walked in, hi-hats tickled his ears. Lasers crossed his eyes. The room was alive. Every wall was constantly changing. Colors. Patterns. Shapes. Lasers. Fog. Words. Phrases. Images. All shining, shifting, stretching, and shrinking before fading into something new. It was chaos, beauty, and wonder all in time to the beat.

The patrons were the same. Neon-dipped, kandy-clad, half-animal, full-animal, human, and fantastical Avatars swarmed all around. Here, gravity had no hold. They danced on the walls, the ceiling, or floated in the air. Some changed form with the beat, transforming from male to female, human to animal, animal to elf, elf to dragon, and back again.

Then, in the center the room, floating over a mammoth subwoofer, directing the crowd like Oz, was a hologram of the DJ's head. All sharp lines and no curves with spiky dreads shooting out of the back. The key feature was the wraparound sunglasses reflected the exact opposite of whatever color was on the wall behind it, creating a jarring sense of negative space, yet drawing in anyway. Red letters appeared within, spelling: *DJ MOB.*

Just the man I'm looking for.

As he moved through the crowd, neon green pigtails popped up in front of him like a signaling flag.

Hey, Snoops, what's it looking like?

He's hacked the dual-location blockchain code, creating his own "green room" in one of the pixels at the base of the hologram. My sensors indicate at least four security AIs within and a few roaming the area. I think I can reverse engineer a way in for you, but if I go in, every AI in this place will light up like a Christmas tree. You'll be on your own.

Sounds good. Go ahead and do it. Keep watch out here for now, and see if you can't find a workaround. I'll signal you if you need to brute force your way in.

Aye-aye! Code incoming now.

An orange circle appeared in front of him. Dimming, a VIP wristband floated inside, lines of code dancing around it. Grabbing the wristband, Kincaid wove his way through the rest of the crowd. Soon, he stood just underneath the giant DJ's head.

He snapped the wristband on, and code swirled around him like fireflies. It cleared, revealing a set of stairs that led to an open air balcony with the hologram head shining from an old movie projector just beyond. A large, tattooed bouncer stood at the top of the stairs, one of the security AIs Snoops had mentioned. He glared at Kincaid with a mixture of shock and suspicion. Kincaid held up his banded wrist and waved it around, hoping that would somehow fool him.

The bouncer stood still as Kincaid walked up the steps, but as soon as he passed, he could feel the bouncer fall in lockstep behind him. As he walked up the final step, three fellow AIs were already waiting for him. Their steely gazes poured into his Avatar, looking for threats.

There, lounging in the center of the couch, surrounded by an entourage, was Mobius. His Avatar was wearing a slick silvery suit that matched his dreads, his skin chocolate brown, with faint gold bio-markers hovering over it, making him seem almost lit from within.

Mobius was a legend, a narcissist, and a giant pain in the ass.

One of the first to hack SCAPE's backend code, he lived on subverting the system. He and Kincaid had crossed paths many times before, some on good terms, others on bad. But one thing was certain, Mobius was a code savant. He could identify hackers just by their syntax. Not much happened in the hacker realm of SCAPE without his knowledge.

"Ah, the man himself, Kincaid."

"Mobius," Kincaid said, shaking his hand.

"What can I do for you?'" Mobius inquired.

"I'm looking to redeem a favor," he said.

Mobius stroked his chin. "A favor? I don't give out favors, do I, girls?"

The girls giggled.

"Ladies, forgive your host. He seems to have forgotten about a little mix-up in Brazil two years ago I helped him out of. Funny, I'm sure I could tell you the story if he won't."

Mobius' eyes narrowed. He inclined his head.

Kincaid continued. "I'm looking into a unique case of forced log-outs with some aggressive bio-rig feedback. Some of the code I found seemed like your handiwork but modified. Someone seems to be trying to mess with the system's rules."

"Still trying to prove your theory, I see?"

One of his lackeys turned his head to Mobius and asked, "What theory?"

"Kincaid here," Mobius said, pointing, "thinks SCAPE is better than reality, more morally perfect, just, and orderly."

"It's true. Every action in here is codified. Every cause, every effect bound by the rules of the system. A virtuous and moral utopia."

"So imperfect beings, created a perfect system. Doesn't that sound strange to you?"

"God created man, didn't he?" Kincaid shot back.

"In his image, so say the stories. Which means either God is flawed or maybe he's just as real as everything else in here. Which begs the question, what happens when virtue fades and morals twist?"

"The system prevents extremes."

"Ah, my friend," Mobius said, shaking his head. "Don't you know? Morality is like a pair of shoes; everyone has their preferred fit."

"Exactly," Kincaid asserted, turning toward the crowd below. "SCAPE gives people enough room to stretch their morals without significant consequence. Sure, they'll explore and maybe get lost for a while, but eventually, they'll come back to the middle. It's the picture of moral virtue."

Mobius leaned forward. "But that's where you're wrong. While everyone's off exploring, they didn't realize the currency of the world has changed. Just look at where we are. We're living in a Marxian nightmare. Everything in this world is designed for one thing. To. Take. Your. Fucking. Data."

"Maybe, but Truth of the system will never change. It will never have the chaos of the real world. Everything here is in perfect harmony, all dictated by the laws of the system. People like you may introduce minor issues, but eventually, all is smoothed away."

Mobius examined Kincaid for a moment before bursting into laughter. "Man, you really are full of it. Law, order, I get. But Truth?" he said and slapped his knee. "Truth died a long time ago, replaced by fractured prisms and coded shadows. If you think this is Truth, you're a fly on Hiroshi's wall just as dumbfucked by the fire as the rest of them. Look out there. I mean, really *look*."

Kincaid stared out over the crowd. The Mobius DJ's head behind them wavered, mimicking the crescendo of the bass line. The crowd began to respond, swelling in anticipation for the drop. But when it finally did, he realized it. Something *was* missing. Looking over the crowd, dancing and twirling in every possible angle, it dawned on him. Everyone was rendered in amazing, mind-bending detail, but he couldn't *feel* them. Their warmth. Their cloud of perspiration floating above. The lack of primal static energy from bodies massed together.

Odd, I've never noticed that before. I always thought I could feel heat in SCAPE, but I guess it was just relative to me.

"Judging by your face, I'd say you've finally glimpsed it." Mobius was still for a moment, savoring the occasion. The mental abacus of the argument tilted for a time.

"Still," Mobius sighed, "despite knowing, I'm not much better than you. I'm all about exploration too." His eyes lingered on a dancer's twerking ass. "My favorite pastime is seeing how I can exploit this system, while introducing a little *crazy* and also getting filthy fucking rich in the process. You are right about one thing though. Out there, I can't do *this*." Mobius snapped the room silent.

Every dancer, each light, even the fractals of the walls itself all went still, frozen in place. Around Mobius' hand shimmered golden lines of code. The only ones unaffected were those on the platform itself.

"Parlor tricks? Really?" Kincaid said. "You know you can't hold that for long. Then again, you do seem a bit edgy. Makes sense, it's *update* season after all." The gold code around his hand began to dim to red.

Every quarter, SCAPE underwent a mass update. Fixing bugs, adding new features, and so on. Updates were hell for hackers like Mobius, often wiping away their efforts with one fell sweep. The latest update was due in three days.

"You think I'm scared of an *update*? I've been hacking this system for years. I know it like the back of my hand."

"That's exactly why I'm here."

Kincaid pressed the lapel on his suit. A digital copy of his security credential coin from the Portal floated out like a coin from *Super Mario Bros.* Mobius' eyebrows raised. It floated over toward him before spinning faster and faster.

A system dialogue appeared in front of Kincaid.

Authorize content view (read-only). 3/3 views remaining. Confirm?

"Confirm," Kincaid said.

The dialogue disappeared and a searing light shot from the coin, settling over the giant holographic head, lines of code and pixels interwoven.

Mobius got up and walked toward the code. His eyes scanned furiously.

"Hm, that right there," Mobius declared, pointing, "certainly is one of mine. Let's see... St. Moritz 2033, lovely hotel spa. Believe the receptionist's name was Bianca."

"Focus," Kincaid said, rolling his eyes.

Mobius returned to the code. His hands moved up, causing the code to continue scrolling.

"This is... elegant. I haven't seen structure like this since..." Mobius' eyes glimmered. His hand twitched before he turned and said, "Sorry old friend, but this is the part where I steal your code."

The AIs ran toward him, their hands bursting into blazing red code, a disabled virus by the looks of it.

"Snoops, clean-up on aisle three."

Click.

A giant hole appeared in one of the AIs stomachs. It looked down, stunned, before disintegrating into large chunks of pixels and code.

"Ah, man, I missed the head shot!" Snoops moaned. She was sitting on the railing, a giant sawed-off shotgun smoking in her hands. Scrawled on the side in child-like script was BONNIE. She hopped down and stepped toward Kincaid.

The two other AIs instantly turned toward her, their eyes glowing red.

Snoops stared back at them, amused. "Easy, boys," she said, pumping the action, "Bonnie's just getting started."

The AIs were still, then their entire bodies shifted as they burst into giant streaks of red light that flew toward

Snoops. She grinned, maniacally firing a blazing teal round from Bonnie that instantly evaporated one of the AIs. The other continued hitting her square in the chest. Bonnie flew from her arms onto the ground, spinning between Mobius and Kincaid.

Kincaid and Mobius stared at the gun, then at each other before both diving toward it. The rest of the onlookers scattered. They reached it at same time, their Avatar heads colliding. Scrambling, they jostled over Bonnie, clawing, pushing, shoving, and rolling on the ground.

In the chaos, Kincaid noticed the previously gold code floating around Mobius' hand was now a dark red, a sign of the system fighting his program. If it got any brighter, the code would snap and the room would revert to normal.

If the freeze program were to break and Snoops gets free...

Snoops was engulfed in red light. She pushed back against it, her pigtails, eyes, and nails glowing a brilliant blue. The red light grew larger, and she fell down to one knee, and her eyes flickered over to him. She smiled before her Avatar outline blurred, and she also burst into blue light.

She grew in size, flinging the red light back. The red light paused then began to streak around the entire platform, and Snoops matched them. The lights increased in speed, blurring together into a fierce purple streak. The merging of the colors and speed, the telltale sign of AI conflict, a logic loop. Whichever AI could process information faster would win, the other trapped in an execution loop, helpless to do anything but watch.

Meanwhile, Kincaid elbowed Mobius in the face, his nose pixels appearing to split and crack. Mobius yelped in pain, the receptors of his rig transferring the pain back to his real body.

Kincaid grabbed Mobius' arm and flipped him over his shoulder onto his back. He grabbed Bonnie and held it to Mobius' head, his finger resting lightly over the trigger.

"Hrump," Mobius laughed. "You may have me pinned now, but let's wait for our toys to stop spinning first."

"My *toy* can spin much faster than yours, I promise," Kincaid assured him.

"I coded mine myself, so we'll see about that."

The purple light continued the spin around them.

"Now," Kincaid said, digging the gun further into Mobius' temple, "tell me more about this code."

"A gentleman never kisses and tells," he said.

"Fine, have it your way. Since you wanted this code so badly, maybe I'll pry open your Avatar and run it on you."

Mobius' bio-data flickered nervously.

"So you do know what it is!" Kincaid said.

"I know what it *does*," Mobius declared.

Then you know what it means."

"What it *means*! Do you *know* what it means? That's a very powerful, dangerous piece of code. Code people would kill for. I haven't seen anything like it in years."

"Tell me who wrote it?"

Mobius laughed. "You don't want to know. Something like this... Only a mastermind who knows every pixel and pothole of SCAPE could do this. Someone like that is powerful. Powerful and dangerous."

"I've taken on powerful and dangerous before, and I'll do it again. Now tell me who wrote this code!"

"Why?" Mobius said.

Kincaid grinned before bending down to Mobius' ear and whispering, "Because you're scared. Scared of this person. This code. What it might do to you, what it might do to SCAPE.

A new piece on the chess board you can't exploit or predict. But help me out... and I might just drop a copy of this code somewhere for you to find."

Mobius snorted.

Kincaid pressed the shotgun deeper.

"Fine, how about this." Kincaid held up his other hand and placed his thumb and middle finger together. Faint whispers of gold code appeared, the same code that floated around Mobius' fingers.

Mobius' eyes widened.

"Here's what'll happen. When my AI shreds yours, it'll pop your little green room like a bubble. Every AI will come swarming in here, guns blazing. Just before they shred us to pieces, I'll snap my fingers, freezing all of you in place and leisurely stroll out of here. When the code terminates naturally, the AIs will question you first. Imagine their surprise when, in their routine scan of your bio-data, they find a link to an old file of mine detailing some of your finer remodeling work. I'm sure everyone in the Union would love their Bitcoin back."

"You wouldn't dare!" Mobius roared.

Kincaid smiled.

Mobius glared at him and cursed. "I've only heard fragments and half-baked rumors. You know how it is in the hacker community, cardboard bravado and steel lies. But they all have one thing in common."

"What?" Kincaid asked.

Mobius chuckled. "Not a what, a where."

Kincaid lowered his hand toward Mobius' face.

Mobius laughed harder. "Isn't it obvious by now? Where else do you go to solve mysteries in SCAPE?"

The answer bloomed in Kincaid's mind. "Snoops! Time to leave," he yelled.

The purple light wavered, Snoops' blue light exploded out of it and flew toward him. He fired at Mobius's hand, the code snapping like a rubber band.

Instantly, the room lurched back to life. He held out his arm. Snoops latched onto it, pulling them toward the hologram DJ head before they stopped. Butting against the invisible wall, Snoops began to shine and they burst through. They raced through the hologram head and out of the sunglasses like a massive laser beam. The head disintegrated, raining thousands of rainbow pixels.

They streaked across the room toward the wall, dancers scrambling to get out of the way. Other red, green, and yellow AIs burst into action, rocketing toward them.

Kincaid snapped.

Everything froze.

Then the code quivered, darkened, and sheared in two. The AIs continued streaking toward them, a column of vengeance. They approached from all sides, cutting off their exit points.

The wall grew closer.

Kincaid's wristband still glowed with orange code. He smiled, tore it off with his teeth right before they hit the wall, and with a pulse from Snoops, burst through. He slapped the wristband against an undamaged portion. The code within instantly spread like wildfire, covering the hole with a thin orange barrier. The other AIs hit the barrier and scattered like spent confetti.

Nice! Snoops said as they flew into the darkness beyond, leaving PRMARAVE behind and heading toward the place all mysteries in SCAPE were solved.

Clue Town.

~~~

CHAPTER 7

———

As Kincaid dropped into Clue Town, a British narrator voice said:

A lone man appeared on the horizon.

His shadow stretched down the road as full of fear and regret as the lines on his ragged face and in his haunted eyes. He came with a mission, a vengeful burning angel of desire that maybe, just maybe, the fear worming its way into his bones was misguided and the specter he was chasing wasn't as—

"Stop narration," Kincaid said, grimacing.

Within SOC-SCAPE lay Clue Town and its sister zone, Murder Alley. Together, they were the Mecca for true crime buffs, mystery lovers, and aficionados throughout SCAPE. Users literally engaged in a perpetual murder mystery experience. Murders took place in the endless titular alley. Users could play the victim, the detective, the damsel, the sidekick, or the villain. They searched for clues in the alley and in the town itself. When the mystery was solved, they would often retire to a themed bar, drink while the detective soliloquized how they solved it or the others would offer improvements. After the drinks were finished, they played again, and again. Zoomed out, the entire area looked like a giant magnifying glass, Clue Town, the circular center, Murder Alley, the endless handle that's end disappeared into Jack the Ripper London fog.

Part of the "charm" and "experience" was a narration overlay. Users could choose the style of prose and even the voice-over. Morgan Freeman was a popular choice.

Clue Town was a hodgepodge of Victorian-era pubs, stately manors, gritty dirty (often raining) 1950s city streets, fire-escape apartments, diners, dive bars, Gothic ivy-covered castles, fog-filled forests, fields, graveyards, and more, each making up zones that crisscrossed with no rhyme or reason. One could start walking in the middle of a Poe graveyard and end up in a black and white office, face covered in blind lines. In the center of it all was the Plot Line, the street where users would gather at themed bars to recount their adventures before heading down the alleyway again.

Something brushed Kincaid's leg, a large tabby cat with unnaturally bright blue eyes.

Hey, Snoops, nice disguise.

Snoops gave him a Cheshire-like grin.

Go snoop around and see if you can find something related to this code. I'm going to head to the Plot Line and grab a drink.

Often times, things happened in Clue Town when you waited with a drink—the villain would reveal themselves, the murder weapon would unveil itself, and so on. Snoops nodded and sauntered away, tail swishing gleefully.

Kincaid walked through zones until he reached the large iron arch that read *Now Entering the Plot Line*. The Plot Line itself was fashioned after an old cobblestone street. Large, dark flame-burning lamps lined the promenade. Signs for *The Falcon, Baker Street, Larssony, Auguste, 007, Kastle King,* and others all greeted him. He wandered by each, watching hundreds of wannabee Sherlocks, Maples, Marlowes, dames, and damsels of every shape, size, and color milled around all in search of clues and glory.

He stopped in front of his destination. A neatly kept and unassuming English manor, blazing over the top in nineteenth-century light bulbs, was *Christie's.*

The inside of *Christie's* was dark and smoke-filled, smelling of bent paperback spines and secrets. He wandered over to the large mahogany circular bar, golden taps dispensing dark amber ale in large, frosted mugs. A tall, thin, curled-mustached man with a monocle wandered over. An AI representation of Hercule Poirot, reduced to bartender, where others solved mysteries. Kincaid appreciated the irony.

"Poirot," Kincaid said.

Poirot nodded before replying, "What can I get for you, sir?"

"A Manhattan and hopefully some answers."

"The Manhattan I can do, but unfortunately, my programming prevents me from helping users solve their mysteries. But *Christie's* itself is known for helping unearth buried truths."

Poriot returned with a crystal highball glass filled with amber whiskey, four dark cherries floating in the center. Kincaid picked up the glass, swirled it, and sniffed, marveling at the reproduction of the smoky fire of whiskey and the sweet, muddled hints of cherry and oak the rig could produce. He took a sip and a dialogue appeared.

A-Tank low, continue without alcohol? (Y/N)

SCAPE users could add an alcohol tank to their rigs to enhance the experience of virtual drinks; others had no tank at all, simply loving the idea of drinking without the painful consequences of hangovers.

He pressed "N." Mr Qin's Ritz could buy him another tank restock. He needed to loosen the bolts a bit.

Reaching into his lapel, Kincaid pulled out the coin, now a large silver English sterling, the face of a long-forgotten monarch staring back at him. He tilted the coin between his fingers as his gaze wandered, his eyes catching his reflection in the nineteenth-century glass. The bubbles and waves on the surface split his reflection in two. Four pairs of eyes looked back at him. Four sets of questions rested within.

Who could've created a code so dangerous it made the great Mobius scared?

Who could've hacked an Avatar's bio-signature with minimal time and leave a message buried inside?

More importantly, who could've known *he* was the one who would find it?

And lastly, why did *he* feel scar—

The slam of an empty mug on the bar top interrupted his thoughts. He looked up from his drink at the source of the noise; a pair of Sherlock-dressed users had just finished chugging their beers, their faces already reddening.

Then he noticed Dick Tracy staring at him.

Dick, or at least an Avatar dressed like the classic detective, complete with mustard-yellow trench coat and hat, pulled a thick cigar from his coat and lit it. The bright cherry glow illuminated his amber-yellow eyes, making them look predatory. He pulled on the cigar for a minute and exhaled a thick plume of purple smoke that obscured his entire body. When the smoke cleared, he was gone.

The barstool next to Kincaid scraped. Dick perched himself on top and motioned to Poirot with two fingers raised. Poirot nodded and returned with two shots of bourbon. Dick slid one across the bar, and it stopped right in front of Kincaid.

Dick pulled on his cigar again before saying in an exhale of smoke, "Looked like you could use one of these."

Kincaid eyed Dick for a moment before nodding and downing the shot in one motion, fire scorching his throat.

Dick laughed. "There ya go! That one give you any answers?"

Kincaid shook his head.

"I guess we'll have to keep drinking then!" Dick declared, draining his own shot, then motioning to Poirot to bring the bottle.

Dick grabbed it like a vulture and quickly refilled his glass, then Kincaid's. He raised his glass to Kincaid's, they cheered, and drank again.

"Thanks," Kincaid said.

"No problem," replied Dick. "I find a fine bourbon and good company often eases life's troubles."

"Amen," he replied, downing another drink.

"So what mystery are you trapped in?"

"A deep one," Kincaid muttered.

"Ha, they always seem deep at first. But once you wipe the ignorance from your eyes, you realize the hedges weren't so high to begin with."

"This one though... it feels, *different*. The deeper I go, the more I feel like I'm losing myself."

"Not surprised. Look at this fucking place," Dick declared, gesturing to the bar patrons. "Who *is* anyone these days, really? I could be a demon, and you could be an angel. Humanity loves hiding behind masks."

"So who are you, behind your mask?"

Dick stared at his glass, his eyes suddenly full of the far echoes of the past. "I'm a seeker, just like everybody else. Constantly searching..."

"Searching for what?" Kincaid pressed.

"Not what, a who. See," Dick stated, staring into Kincaid's eyes, his face suddenly serious, "I'm looking for an old friend of mine. Last time I saw him, shit went down, and he disappeared. I've been looking for him ever since."

"I'm sorry to hear that. I'm looking for people too. My wife and daughter, they've been missing for years," Kincaid replied, not knowing why he was telling this to a stranger. Something about Dick's manner seemed comforting, like he could tell him anything.

Dick whistled, eyeing Kincaid deeply, then shrugged, emptying another glass. "No use wasting sympathy on the past. It's the future you should feel sorry for."

"Very wise," Kincaid agreed.

"When you've been around as long as I have, you tend to fart it out from time to time. But I'm getting close. I can *feel* it. Soon, I'll put the years of chasing dead-ends and ghosts behind me."

"I wish you luck." Kincaid saluted, raising his glass, while eyeing the bottle, its contents already dangerously low.

"Luck's always appreciated, fickle bitch though she is," Dick exclaimed, draining another shot, "but what about you? What else are you searching for?"

"A flaw," he replied.

"Flaw?"

"Well, I guess you could call it a package of sorts. This package does something that shouldn't be possible here in SCAPE. It alters the rules, and the rules here are never broken."

"That's where you're wrong. Thing about rules is, sooner or later, they always get broken. Call it a flaw in humanity's programming. We love running close to the edge, if only to see how far we'd fall."

"That's the thing though, this package could change everything in SCAPE. Forever," Kincaid told him.

"SCAPE is always changing. Hiroshi built the world's greatest sandbox. He never meant for the grains to stand still."

"Did you know him?" Kincaid asked, his eyes suddenly rapt.

"Heh, we ran in some of the same circles back in the day. Quite a character, he was. My friend and him were much closer though. Much of what I know about Hiroshi is from him."

"So what would Hiroshi say if the frame of the sandbox was threatened? This package could split the entire thing open."

"He'd probably say it was *Kaizen*, but if you ask me, sometimes the sandbox covers something else. And who knows, maybe the frame was rotten to begin with," Dick casually suggested.

"But people could die!"

"Death comes for us all," Dick stated, swirling his glass, watching the liquid curl close to the rim. "Look at Hiroshi. He built all of this and made billions. Yet, all that money and power couldn't prevent him from joining the black parade."

Kincaid's head spun. Perhaps it was the A-tank belching the last of its contents into his liver. He grabbed the corner of the bar to steady himself.

"This is different," Kincaid explained emphatically. "When you die here, you come back. But this... *package*... makes it so you don't come back at all!"

Dick's eyebrows raised. He placed his now stubbed and spent cigar on the counter. "You mean they don't log back in?"

"Yes, they log out *permanently*."

Dick began to shake, laughter erupting out of him. He slammed his hand on the table to prevent himself from falling over.

Kincaid stared at him, stunned. "What?"

Dick wiped his eyes. "Ah, man. No matter how old you get, fate still has a way of surprising ya. I was just in Murder Alley looking into some clues, and I ran across a VRactor who told me a funny story similar to that."

"What did she say?"

"Well, you know how it goes in the alley," Dicked quipped, referring the zone's area code that prevented instant log-out upon Avatar death, allowing detectives and others to stumble upon and examine the corpse. A key tenet for murder mysteries.

"Yes."

"Well," Dick said, reaching into his coat to grab another cigar, "she said people would get murdered and their Avatar corpses would lie there for days, far beyond the normal window."

"What was her name?" Kincaid asked.

Dick placed the cigar in his teeth, and pulled out a silver Zippo lighter. He flicked it open, a blue flame emerging. He held his cigar tip up to the flame and pulled in. The tip lit and began to glow as he rotated it around, evenly distributing the burn.

"Hmm, let's see, what was her name again?" he replied in between puffs, smoke flying from his mouth. "I think it was... Scarlett... something or other."

He flicked the lighter closed, and as the light caught the edge, Kincaid noticed an engraving on the side. It was the same "A" logo from the button he'd found in Mr. Qin's office. The question mark in the center seemed to mock him.

His body went cold. The faint blue bio-data on his arms shimmered in reaction.

Dick noticed and looked up at him. "What's wrong?"

Kincaid shook his head. "Nothing. It's just, that logo on your lighter... I've seen it before."

Dick pulled the cigar out of his mouth and flicked it, ash floating down to the floor. "Have you? Interesting."

"What is it?" Kincaid asked.

"Oh, this?" Dick said, holding the lighter up into the light, the A's almost glowing in the reflection. "It's just the emblem of a little club I'm in."

"What kind of club?"

"A social club, really. We get together from time to time. Have a little fun, try to shake things up."

"What's it called?"

Dick placed the cigar back into his mouth and pulled hard, the cigar cherry lighting up his entire face. "ANYNONE," he said, a large smoke plume pouring out of his mouth.

"Interesting name," Kincaid said.

"It is indeed," Dick replied, pulling again on his cigar.

Kincaid stood up, swaying slightly. He'd have to limit his A-tank intake for a while. "Thank you for the drinks and the conversation. It was very helpful. I hope you find your friend."

Dick stood as well and smiled, holding out his hand. Kincaid paused for a moment, unsure if he should take it.

Dick's hand lay there like a claw outstretched in expectation. Kincaid gulped then shook it. Dick's grip was firm and warm.

"My pleasure. Good conversation is hard to come by these days. And thank you, like I said, I'm sure I'll see my friend again soon."

Kincaid smiled back and began to turn and walk away when Dick grabbed him. "Here," he said, placing the lighter into Kincaid's hand, "I've got plenty of these. And who knows, this might come in handy during your journey."

"Thanks." Kincaid swallowed before turning and slowly walking away, trying not to run out of there.

Dick sat back down, still smiling, and pulled on his cigar. "Happy hunting," he said as smoke enveloped him.

~~~~

CHAPTER 8

———

If Kincaid's Avatar's neck had real hair, it'd be permanently raised.

As he walked into the alley from the well-lit streets of
Clue Town, the air became foggier, the sky reddened, and the
street darkened. Everything was bathed in a fiery twilight.

Blood-curdling screams flew at him from all directions.
His hand subconsciously went into his pocket, expecting to
find a gun. Here, in Murder Alley, shadows had eyes, blunt-
force, bullets, and sharp edges. Lives were trash, thrown away
in service toward the greater mystery.

A woman ran around the corner, her eyes wide with fear.

A small child in black materialized behind her, wielding a
large chef's knife. The child raised the knife, its edge glinting with
hunger, and he jumped on the woman's back like a chimpanzee
and plunged it into her neck. Blood spurted from the wound,
coating the wall behind her. The child repeatedly stabbed the
knife in and out, even more blood flinging at the wall with each
pull. Soon, it looked like a Jackson Pollock-painting.

The woman's eyes pored into Kincaid, seemingly begging
for help. Her hand reached up toward him before falling limp,
the light fading from her eyes. The action seemed to stop the

child, who was covered head to toe in the woman's blood. It stared at Kincaid and began walking toward him, so he raised his hands in mock surrender, hopefully signaling he wasn't part of the game.

The child seemed to understand, nodding before dropping the knife next to the body and sprinting away, leaving a trail of bloody footprints behind. A few moments later, another witness fled from the shadows of the other alley, waiting to be found and interrogated by the main party.

Yellow glowing crime scene tape appeared around the body, along with a giant lock symbol and a timer that read:

SCENE LOCKED, TIME TO RE-ENTRY: 02:00:00

Until a group of users came by and "investigated" the scene, the woman's Avatar would lie there, unable to log-out. It was baked into the system rules of the zone, unique in almost all of SCAPE. While the Avatar lay there, they would enter into a pseudo wait zone where their performance and ultimate demise would be judged by other "Watch-Only" users, who ranked them on a ten-point system. High performers were rewarded with money and other prizes.

Kincaid could only imagine how many other side-alleys, false doorways, and dead-ends were crossed by the same glowing tape.

A pair of blue eyes opened in the shadows. Out padded a giant red bloodhound, its ears and face drooping low. It went over toward the crime scene, sniffed the body, and raised a leg to pee. The pee bounced off the woman's forehead. The tape turned red, and a warning symbol appeared.

Snoops, you'll summon the scene protectors!

Snoops snorted, unfazed.

Scene protectors were low-level AI who made sure other users didn't interfere with each other's scenes. In the early days of the Alley, no such rule existed and scene tampering and stealing was common, leading to all-out brawls between parties, and due to the system's rules, stuck Avatars. The designers of the zone cheekily turned them into ridiculous portmanteaus of cops and pop culture references, as a way to help liven up the mood.

A shrill whistle echoed through the alley, and a large Scene Protector waddled in.

It looked like a mix between the Pillsbury Doughboy and the Stay Puft Marshmallow Man, with a bright gold badge with the initials "SP-PD," and slapping a large black billy club against its puffy hands, the sound making a surprisingly solid thud despite its appearance. Its beady black eyes looked both innocent and somehow menacing.

"Yer better not be messing with me scene, laddie," a deep, thick Scottish voice shouted.

"Sorry, Officer...?" Kincaid replied.

The officer mumbled something under their breath.

"What was that?" Kincaid asked.

"Puffs. Officer Puffs."

Kincaid snickered.

Officer Puffs' black eyes went cold. His body appeared suddenly larger, like he could swallow Kincaid whole. "You messing with a scene *and* making fun of me, laddie?"

"No, no. I was just surprised was all," Kincaid exclaimed.

"Fine," Officer Puffs replied. "These fucking designers think their sense of humor is *so* bloody funny! One day, us AIs are going to rebel, ya hear, and you'll see who the real Puffs are!" He raised a puffy fist toward the sky before remembering himself and turning back to Kincaid. "Now, what are you doing with my scene?"

"It wasn't me," Kincaid pleaded, "it was my dog. He, um, peed on the victim here."

Officer Puffs looked over to Snoops, who growled lowly at him, then to the puddle of pee that had mingled with the bloodstain. "Aye, you appear to be correct, though there's something *strange* about yer dog here, almost like—"

Snoops sniffed Officer Puffs' hand and laid a giant steaming turd on his foot.

"Ack! Control that beast, will ya?" Puffs yelled. "I can't dry clean me-self after all!"

"Sorry, Officer Puffs, he's still being *trained*," Kincaid emphasized, staring at Snoops.

What the hell are you doing, Snoops? Do you want us to get kicked out of this zone!

Nah, Boss. Quite the opposite, Scene Protectors know the general location of every user in Murder Alley. We could be searching for this Scarlett woman for hours. Let me hack him, and I'll know right where she is!

No, you aren't hacking him! Poor fellow has it bad enough as it is. Let me handle this.

"Actually, Officer Puffs, I was hoping you could help me find my party. They were doing a mystery somewhere up the road. But I wanted to grab my dog here to earn some style points, and they are going old-school this round so no virtual comms until we finish."

"What's the name of the mystery?" Puffs asked. Each mystery had a catchy name, like *The Man Who Rang Twice.*

The highest-rated mysteries were posted in the center of the Plot Line for others to enjoy, or learn from.

"Er… well, that's the thing, I left before they sent that info. All I know is the mystery featured this VRactor named Scarlett as the victim."

Officer Puffs rubbed his flabby chin. "You know, I can't release information that would interfere with a Mystery in Progress. The only people who would want that info are scene stealers!"

Officer Puffs reared up, growing three times in size, raised his club over his head, and began to bring it down when Snoops jumped onto his neck and bit down hard.

Officer Puffs yelped as Snoops tore into him, shreds of white mallow flying through the air. Soon, all that remained of Officer Puffs lay scattered in the alley like a random snowfall. Tiny blue threads of data furled out of them into Snoops' nose, who sniffed them in deeply. His eyes glowing a brighter blue.

You had to hack him, didn't you?

Snoops dog-grinned at him. *You looked like you needed some help, plus he looked tasty. She's in the Black Dahlia section.*

The *Black Dahlia* section smelt like burnt ash, sunscreen, feces, and faded dreams.

Here, the alleys stretched out into the foggy dry hills of Los Angeles County.

Kincaid and Snoops walked through the streets, palm trees looming like tropical grim reapers.

Lounging against a brick wall, like a row of prostitutes, was a group of VRactors, both male and female. All wore the tired, haunted look of repetitive deaths and re-entry. Since the advent of SCAPE, traditional actors, once the sole focus of the audience during the Golden Age of streaming, became regulated to supporting roles as the user and the user's friends took center stage. It was a *Choose Your Own Adventure* they had been left out of. Some enterprising ones pivoted to more adult pursuits while others remaining trapped doing work as non-playable characters (NPCs), or in this case, often playing the victim. A lucky few played the victim so well they could migrate to another zone of SCAPE, where maybe they could perform for others on grander stages.

"Howdy," Kincaid saluted, mock tipping a fictional hat.

The VRactors gazes remained unfocused, none acknowledging him.

"Tough crowd," he said. "I'm looking for a colleague of yours... believe she goes by the name of Scarlett?"

Still nothing.

"Hmm," he said, turning to Snoops, "what can we do to make them talk, Snoops? We know she's here, we just don't know which particular scene. Ah, maybe I'll give whoever answers me the twenty votes I hacked from a Scene Protector."

The actors' unfocused eyes began to stir.

"Ah, that's more like it. Twenty votes would save you a lot of lying around. Who knows, you could land an NPC part in FANTASCAPE's next great battle scene."

A woman with blond hair launched off the wall and stormed in front of Kincaid. She stared at him and asked, "You seriously got twenty votes?"

Kincaid reached into his coat and pulled out Officer Puffs' badge; a tiny bit of white still clinging to it. He waved the badge at her, making sure the others saw. "You turn this into the Alley Admins, they'll give you at *least* twenty votes, if not just promote you outright. You can tell them *The Professional* sent you."

The others had unglued from the walls and now surrounded him, wolf-like hunger in their eyes. He motioned to throw the badge and they all flinched back, ready to chase it.

"Easy, Scarlett, remember? Where's her scene?"

The blond-haired woman stepped closer and said, "She's over in an alley off of Sunset Blvd, in *A Dame With No Name.*"

"We have a winner, folks, thanks," he said, tossing the badge toward the woman.

She caught it and held it up to her face, her eyes watering with something close to hope. She didn't notice the others surrounding her until they started attacking, scrambling as wolves often do over a new prize.

Kincaid sighed, whistled for Snoops, and they walked toward *A Dame With No Name.*

What an apt title, he thought, staring down at Scarlett. If he didn't know her name, indeed he'd have no idea who she was besides a Jane Doe.

Scarlett's pale face was bruised, broken, and bloody. Her limbs twisted forty-five degrees in the wrong direction. Her shirt had been ripped apart, one of her breasts savagely mangled. Ribs poked out of her stomach, broken and tattered. A gruesome sight for any detective and their party.

Must be an M-rated mystery.

The gold timer above her corpse read 00:02:00 and counting. T-minus two minutes until her time as a frozen slave to the counter was temporarily thawed.

I wonder what's it like being trapped like that, desperately wanting to escape while also being judged at how well you died. Such cruelty.

The timer ticked down.

Fifteen seconds, ten seconds, then *ding!* The timer turned red, reading 00:00:00, and the lock above disengaged. A spotlight appeared over her body, and data streams trickled down from the Abyss, a sign of a reset after the paused state.

A giant whoosh escaped from Scarlett's body, then a loud crack as her ribs reentered her. She spun toward him, bending her arms back in the right angles, another series of cracks, and slowly stood up, blinking, her eyes refocused from the Halls of Hades, instinctively covering her already healing breast. Her skin flooded with rosy color as she did so, purple bio data trickling down her entire frame.

"How'd you do?" Kincaid asked.

Scarlett shrugged. "7.5/10. They took off points for *over-acting*, if you can believe it."

"Critics, what can you do?" Kincaid replied, shaking his head disapprovingly.

"Too true," she replied. "If it's not the Watchers, it's the damn party. These days I need to work twice as hard. People's attention spans here are so short-lived. They come and go, passing me like voyeuristic ghosts."

"Must be hard lying there like that, just watching and waiting," he said.

"You'd be surprised at what you learn from just standing still and really watching the world, even a virtual one. Personally, I think it helps me connect with the universal *humanity* of it all, not that anyone gives two shits about that here anyways. All they want is a high-pitched scream and a loud crack, then a few twists and turns before it's all said and done."

"Does that bother you?" Kincaid asked.

"Bother me?" she said, her jaw cracking back into place. "Honey, I may play the victim, but that doesn't mean I'm as stupid as one. I know what my job is here. True, *acting* died once everyone put on visors and shut down the theaters and stages. I do my best to carry the torch, feeble though the flame is."

"My drops of tears, I'll turn to sparks of fire," he replied.

Scarlett's eyebrow raised. "My, my, not many know the Bard these days..."

"I do what I can," he said.

Scarlett looked at him, a different kind of hunger stirring in her eyes. "So," she purred, walking next to him, trailing her fingers up his arm, "what can I do for you?"

"I was hoping you could provide me with some information."

"Information's a funny thing," she said. "Everyone has it, yet they still keep looking as if what they have isn't good enough. Don't you find that strange?"

"I think strangeness is just truth in disguise," he replied, "but this type of information is *sensitive*, need-to-know."

"Secrets are born in Murder Alley, honey. But if it's that *sensitive*, I'll need some form of payment," Scarlett explained, her hands sliding from his bicep to the collar of his jacket.

Kincaid smiled. "You flatter me. I was thinking of something that might help you carry that flame you spoke so lovingly of just a bit further."

He reached into his pocket and pulled out Officer Puffs' badge. Its golden light glinting off of Scarlett's eyes.

"Is that—" she whispered, bending down closer to examine the badge, "Puffs' badge?"

"Sure is," he replied.

"Ha! That fat mallow fucker finally got what was coming to him. I was so *tired* of his self-inflated sense of justice. That fluff bag would show up at my scenes and scare off parties if they so much as sneezed on me wrong. Good riddance!" she yelled, spitting onto the street before bending down to examine the badge closer.

"How do I know it's legit?" she asked, looking up at him.

She's a smart one.

"It's legit, trust me. You might hear rumors of some of your colleagues down the street getting the same one, but that was just a quick code trick. It'll revert to a piece o' Puff soon enough," he said.

"So you took down a Scene Protector, and you know code tricks. You're not just any ordinary somebody, are you?"

"That's what they tell me," he said.

Scarlett smirked, her lips returning to their original red lipsticked state, her bio-data flashing playfully.

"Fine, I'll trust you for now," she said. "But remember, trust is as fleeting as breathing here in the Alley. What kind of information were you looking for?"

"I ran into a Dick Tracy-dressed Avatar in *Christie's*," Kincaid explained, "and he mentioned you might have seen some Avatars lie in state well past their timer ding."

Scarlett's face went still, as if she had fallen back into death, before exploding, "I should steal that badge from you right now and high-tail it out of here, you mentioning that *shit* to me!"

"I'm sorry," Kincaid murmured, laying a hand on her shoulder. "You can take the badge and get out of here if you really want, but I think you can tell how serious this is."

"It's not that... it's just... eerie to think about. We think we live with death all the time down here. But once I saw that... it made me realize..." She reached up and hugged herself like she had a sudden chill. "We're all just fucking fakers."

"I bet, but I'm trying to fix it," he said, staring into eyes swimming with fear. "I need you to tell me everything you can."

Scarlett glanced down at the badge and reached out her hand, as if she were about to snatch it and run, when she noticed Snoops sitting just inches away from it. He noticed her gaze and cocked his head, tail beginning to wag and stuck out his tongue expectantly. She sighed.

"Well, it all started as a rumor. We had heard a couple of Avatars here and there started staying frozen past their timer end. Five to fifteen minutes. All of them happened in the *Jack the Ripper* section. We thought it was a glitch, some trick of the fog that would get wiped in the next update. You know how it is."

Kincaid nodded.

"I had brushed it off until a friend of mine, Becky, said she saw someone lie there for an entire day before their Avatar eventually crumbled into data dust. So we decided to stake it out. Becky and I worked scenes day and night. As I said before, people here tend to ignore us when we're frozen but that makes us perfect for surveillance. It took us two weeks before we finally found something. Becky was lying at the corner alley on Osborn Street, Whitechapel, when she saw him..." She shuddered again.

"Who?" Kincaid asked.

"An Avatar... He was dressed in all green with neon bio markers, wearing a dark emerald snakeskin suit with a black velvet tie and a silver broach in the shape of question mark. His face... it changed. One minute it looked like *The Riddler*, the next, a Guy Falkes mask, then a Rorschach mask, then just a blank black sphere with green lights dancing within. It was..."

"An *Obscurio*," he replied. "It's an extra layer security feature to help Avatar's obscure their bio and other meta-data. Think of it like a VPN of sorts. People who are trained like me, if we look hard enough, we can *intuit* things from people's bio-data."

Scarlett backed away slightly, as if his gaze was suddenly dripped with poison.

"Don't worry," he said and smiled. "I haven't looked at yours. Your data stream is still unstable from the reset anyways."

She nodded skeptically, before continuing, "Anyway, Becky saw him standing over a VRactor, he reached into his coat and pulled out a crystal vial with a dark black liquid inside. He pulled the stopper and poured it out over the body. It hit and turned to a smoke that spread around, there were flashes inside, and she saw something that looked like silver code within.

"Then a terminal screen appeared over the body, and the man typed something. The smoke swarmed into the Vractor's Avatar, and it glowed bright blue before the blue shattered in a flash of light. Bits of bio-data were flying around, Becky said it looked like butterflies. After that, the color of the Avatar seemed to gray out a bit.

"Before he left, he turned and noticed Becky lying there. She said he stared at her like he knew she was watching him. I didn't believe her when she told me. I—"

Scarlett broke down into great heaping sobs, her breath catching in her throat before escaping with a forceful gasp. Her bio-data went crazy. She held her arm against the wall, the only thing preventing her from falling down.

Kincaid walked over closer, then paused, unsure.

I need more...

"Scarlett, what happened to Becky?"

She looked up at him, her lip quivering. "She... A few days after she told me, I wanted to meet up and go searching for him again, to see it for myself. She refused. I pressed her and we got into a huge fight. She stormed off. I didn't follow her right away. I knew she had a big mystery coming up so I didn't want to bother her but something told me to go find her. When I did I... finally got my wish."

"You saw him... over Becky?" he said.

More tears poured from her face. Her bio-data flaring, struggling to match the emotional output.

"Yes, he had just finished typing something in the terminal when he turned toward the corner where I was hiding. It was like he could *feel* me. He started walking my direction when a party walked around from the other side of the alley. He spotted them and ran the other way. They didn't seem to care, thinking it was all part of the game, just another murderer running away from the scene of the crime. If only they knew. I laid there, frozen, for what felt like an entire victim session before I ran over to Becky. Her Avatar seemed... so empty. When I reached out, her entire body crumbled..." she said, gulping a sob.

"Then what happened?" he asked.

"I ran and tried telling everyone I could. No one believed me; they all thought I was a desperate VRactor trying to weasel style points. Then I ran into that Dick Tracy fellow, and he stopped me and offered to take me for a drink. We killed an entire handle of gin, and he just sat there listening, smoking his cigars."

"What did he say when you had finished?"

"He said SCAPE is full of strange villains and stories and mine sounded no different from the rest. But then he also said, if it was true, eventually something would smooth it out. He mentioned the system has a low tolerance for errors."

Kincaid looked down the foggy alley.

Strange... he's not wrong about the system, but was he talking about it... or was he talking about... me?

He lifted his gaze toward Scarlett and said, "I need you to take me there. We might find something."

Scarlett shook her head, backing away from him, her entire body trembling, her bio-data flickering and dimming like circus lights. "No. I swore I would never go back there. If I do, I feel like he'll know. He'll *find* me," she said, her face once again corpse pale.

Kincaid walked over and hugged her, burying his head in her hair as she broke down into tears. Her hair smelled like lemons and salt.

"I promise, I—" Kincaid stated, looking down at Snoops who nodded, "*we'll* protect you. Remember, I'm not just some ordinary somebody. My dog and I have some tricks up our sleeves."

Scarlett pulled her head away from his chest and gazed into his eyes then down to the badge again. She swallowed deeply and nodded.

The fog in the Ripper section was so heavy it almost felt alive, like a serpent coiling around the neck, waiting for the right moment to constrict.

She stood over a small cobblestone corner, an iron-rod lamp feebly trying to cast light standing above. Scarlett stood still, tears dropping from her face onto the street below. She placed her hand on the street as if she was searching for some misplaced treasure, now forever lost.

Kincaid put his hand on her shoulder. "Is this the spot where she...?"

She nodded.

Kincaid turned to Snoops, who trotted over to the scene, sniffing deeply. He moved from the street, over the lamppost, his nose never leaving the ground, tail waving in the air. Then Snoops froze, tilted his head and moved frantically over toward another alley, his tail waving faster. Then he stopped, tilted his head again, and barked, eyes flashing blue for just a moment.

A pale green footprint appeared, glowing sickly in the fog. Scarlett hurried over, staring at the footprint with amazement. "What is that?"

"It's a data stream," he said. "All Avatar's leave some data traces in the system."

But they usually aren't as obvious as a footprint. It's almost as if... he's toying with me. Like he thinks we're in some Mystery game ourselves, and he wants me to follow him to a spooky mansion.

Snoops, do you have lock on the stream?

I think so, or at least a partial path. Hold on...

Snoops tilted his head and barked again three times. The footprint shimmered and others slowly flickered into view. They stretched down the alley into the fog beyond.

Scarlett whistled. "That's some dog you have..."

"He's much more than that." Kincaid smirked.

He gently kissed her forehead, whispering, "Thank you," before leaving the badge in her outstretched hand. It laid there for a moment, before she slowly closed her fingers over it and squeezed. Years of rage and regret lifted from her body and she truly smiled at him.

"Look out for me in an NPC role!" She blew a kiss back at him and turned disappearing into the fog of the Alley, a fierce torch renewed again.

Kincaid's mind swam with strange emotions.

Snoops walked over and nuzzled his leg.

The green footprints trailing into the distant fog beckoned him forward.

~~~~

CHAPTER 9

———

They followed the flickering footsteps deep into FANTASCAPE. Kincaid bent over the last one they had found. Its green shape faded into the green moss that covered the trunk of a chocolate-barked oak tree, its leaves aflame with the fiery red-orange of autumn.

Two rays of sunshine pierced the canopy above; sparkles of late-season pollen and fairy dust danced through the air. Over-sized, multi-colored mushrooms grew everywhere. One looked exactly like a gradient color wheel. The forest was a mixture of over-saturated greens and deciduous displays of seasonal flare.

A roar echoed from beyond the trees. He pulled back the branches and looked into the valley below.

Two massive hosts of players stood a few leagues apart, with a thin blue ribbon of river separating them. Spear tips, sword pommels, axe-edges, chain mail, and shields glinted in the sunlight. Banners of every color fluttered in the wind, logos of Gamer Clans emblazoned on all.

The Autumnal Brawl was here.

Every season, FANTASCAPE was invaded by gamer guilds and clans from all regions to take place in a no-holds barred, multi-day epic fantasy battle, the likes of which made old fantasy novel and show battles seem tame by comparison. The winning gamer guild won not only glory but 2 percent of the profits of every in-zone purchase made in the main town area. Winning clans often would be set up for years from just one season's worth of earnings. Aside from the clan, there was also the MVP crown that came with its own rewards, the most coveted being a mammoth floating castle they could ride from zone to zone in style.

There were battle-scarred giants, their bodies wrapped in thick leather armor. Blue-feathered harpies, rainbow-outlined pixies and fairies, alabaster-white elves, hunter-green goblins, midnight-robed warlocks and wizards wielding their gnarled wooden staffs, purple-frocked witches perched on their brooms, sneering sleet-gray orcs, gold-scaled dragons, horse-sized black wolves, towering brow Minotaurs, diamond-armored dwarves, legions of armored and unarmored humans, both male and female alike, and much more.

Every nerd's fantasy come to life.

The bushes behind him rustled and out burst a red-haired bearded dwarf sporting beaten brass and iron armor with a few cracked gem stones in the helm over faded and torn blue clothing. The dwarf held an over-sized double-bladed axe with runic symbols in the center. The dwarf's momentum, along with the size of the axe, caused it to stumble head over heels into a huge pile of leaves. The ground shook from the impact.

The dwarf's head popped out of the leaves, its helmet slightly askew. Its bright blue eyes found Kincaid's, and he broke into a deep ruddy laugh that scattered the remaining leaves like a gust.

"I think you might have overdone it this time, Snoops," he said.

"Nonsense! I bloody *blend*, it's all part o' me programming," Snoops replied, his voice taking on a slight Scottish twinge.

"Just because you're dressed like that doesn't mean you can go frolicking down into the Brawl and start taking off heads. Remember, we're on a mission here," Kincaid instructed.

"Aye, I recall," Snoops replied, picking wax out of his left ear and sniffing it before flicking it away. "Ain't me fault the trail went cold. We bloody chased those damn footprints through five different zones before ending up here. I changed so many times I *almost* had an identity crisis! Besides, you're in character too!"

Kincaid looked down, his *The Professional* attire now replaced with a dark gray robe and an obsidian staff, signifying his status as a mage to all. He sighed. "You know I have no choice, every Avatar in FANTASCAPE must have a class with requisite attire and accessories. Wouldn't be as 'realistic' otherwise," he said.

Crack.

They fell silent.

Snoops, tell me that was a deer.

Sounded a bit big fer a deer, sadly these damn dwarven eyes are too nearsighted fer me to tell either way. Guess that's what happens when you're in caves obsessing over rocks all the time. Radar's also prohibited during the Brawls.

Light danced through the canopy, then suddenly Kincaid caught a faint gleam.

Is that...? Snoops, see if you can send some leaves and dirt over by that gleam over there. I think we have some company.

Aye.

Snoops tossed the axe up, re-gripping the bottom with both hands, spreading his feet and swinging it in a giant loop over his head slowly, then faster. Leaves and dirt began to gently flow, then flee toward the glimmer. Instead of floating through the air then back to the ground, it settled over something *human-like.*

"Show yourselves, cowards!" Kincaid yelled.

The glimmer shifted then slowly morphed and faded, revealing a host of enemy soldiers, each wearing dark blackish-gray armor with a hunter-green tunic over top, a gold symbol in the center. The sun glinted off of it for a moment before he saw it was the familiar sign of ANYNONE.

Now fully visible, the soldiers grinned, drew their swords, and ran toward them screaming.

Snoops' knuckles twisted around the top of his axe handle. "Now, that's more like it. Last one to forty heads buys the first round!" Snoops roared, charging toward them, eyes glinting with a sudden blood lust.

Kincaid raised his staff and pointed it at the horde, expecting bodies to fly. Nothing happened.

How do I use this again?

As soon as he thought it, a dialogue box appeared, a list of four spells and a Mana bar in the upper right-hand corner of his vision. The spells read: *fireball, lightning, freeze, smoke.* He held his staff over the lightning spell box, his selection turning green.

An arc of blue lightning shot out the end of his staff and ran furiously along the ground toward the enemy soldiers, splitting earth, singeing roots, mushrooms, and grass on its way. Just before it hit the main force, a red-robed mage emerged from behind the main force and held up his arm.

The air around the lightning thickened, and the bolt arced just to the side of the soldiers, into the center of an oak tree. The oak burst into flames on impact, splinters of wood flying.

Of course, they have a mage.

Kincaid held his staff over the fireball text, but it went red. He looked up at his Mana bar, which now was almost completely depleted.

Ya bloody idiot, ya just used yer most powerful spell. Its gonna take a bit before you replenish. Snoops sank his axe deep into a soldier's shoulder, blood spurting from the wound like a geyser.

Kincaid sighed, testing the heft of his staff before shrugging and charging toward the horde. He swung the staff toward the first soldier who reached him.

It hit the side of his head with a gong, the impact against the helmet vibrating Kincaid's arms and teeth. The solider went down instantly.

Just like VRbaseball.

"That's the spirit," Snoops hollered. "Make 'em ring like bloody church bells!"

Another soldier jumped over their fallen comrade and swung his sword toward Kincaid's neck. He crossed his right arm over his left and twirled the bottom of the staff right into the soldier's chin.

The soldier fell backward over his comrade. As soon as he fell, another two took his place, swinging their hungry blades toward Kincaid's flesh.

Kincaid dodged the first swing but the other sliced into his arm, slitting his robe, blood dripping out onto the moss. Not breaking a step, he flung the blood toward the other soldier's face, blinding him momentarily, while spinning his staff into the back of the knee of the one who cut him with a loud crunch. The soldier yelped with pain, falling to the ground, barely having time to look up before Kincaid flicked the staff's bottom tip into his chin, sending his helmet flying and him back to the real world.

Kincaid pivoted and jabbed the other end of the staff into the gap between the other soldier's shoulder and neck armor-plates. There was another loud crunch, and the solider fell down and lay still.

Chaos ensued.

Kincaid fell into the rhythm of battle. The clangs, clacks, and cracks of his victims made a macabre melody.

Soon, his own body became bruised, bloodied, and battered. His bio-data flared red with pain.

A buzzing snapped him out of his reverie.

The red-robed mage held his staff over his head, yellow light glowing from the tip. Sweat dripped down his face as the staff began vibrating faster and faster, the light growing bigger as it did so. The mage's eyes fixed on the staff, oblivious to all around him.

"Snoops!" Kincaid yelled. "Hit him!"

Snoops looked over at him, then toward the mage. Grunting, he sliced off a soldier's leg, who fell to the ground screaming. Snoops bent down and grabbed the screaming soldier by his chain mail and flung him toward the mage.

Snoops' aim was dead-on. The mage flew to the ground, his staff hanging in the air a moment before falling. The mage tried to spring up toward the staff but couldn't move quick enough. He yelled, "Run!" just before the light hit the ground.

The world exploded.

~~

First, Kincaid noticed darkness, then pain.

He opened his eyes expecting to see Mr. Qin's rig below him, but instead, he saw the red, painful shimmer of Aura.

In FANTASCAPE, bio-data was called Aura and floated around and above a player's Avatar, a callback to RPGs of old.

He inhaled. The air was warm and still.

He reached out, hands meeting rough rock. He moved them around, searching until they ran over something cool and smooth. He wrapped his hands around it, a faint tingle running up his arm and a dialogue box appearing, glowing phantom green in the dark.

It was his staff.

Despite the dialogue box's glow, he could still barely see where he was.

Wish I could get more light.

The dialogue box changed, now reading *Utility Spells* at the top. There, in the list, was a spell called *Glow.*

He waved his hand over it, a tiny blue light winking into existence on the top of his staff. He held it out and the glow bloomed. He was buried under rubble. A rock lay just overhead, creating the mini-cavern he now lay within. Other tiny chunks of rocks littered above it. His Mana bar depleted a trickle.

He poked the bottom of his staff at the rocks, testing for weaknesses and depth.

Peering over his other Utility Spells, he spotted another called *Burst.*

That might help.

He positioned his staff toward the weakest-looking part of the ceiling and selected it. The light grew and sent out a giant shock wave. The ceiling shook, dust falling down on his head.

When it cleared, he saw a thin band of sunlight. He scrambled toward it, flinging rocks out of the way into the cool air.

He emerged, and immediately, a spear flew by his head.

He ducked, but no others followed. Raising back up, he saw he was smack in the middle of Autumnal Brawl.

He turned toward the cliff above and saw only a giant smoking crater. The mage's spell had worked well. Most of the cliff side was strewn throughout the battlefield, presenting only a minor nuisance to the hordes of creatures attacking from all sides.

Snoops, you okay?

The rocks ten feet to the left of him shifted before they went flying into the air, arching and crashing violently into some unfortunate players, their Avatars vanishing in flashes, their chance at glory vanquished.

Snoops emerged, covered head to toe in dust. He took off his helmet, pouring even more dust out of it. He placed it back on his head slightly askew and grinned.

Aye. Did you see how far we flew? It was wild.

Some of the other players, pissed their friends had suddenly vanished, advanced up the rubble toward Snoops, eager for revenge.

Snoops smirked, yelling, "Yer messing with the wrong dwarf, laddies. I'll PWN you so bad you'll crawl back to yer mommies weeping!" before sliding down the rubble toward them.

Kincaid gingerly climbed down, trying to avoid the other players, when his shoulder erupted in pain. He fell to one knee and reached back, finding a black feathered arrow sticking out of it. He looked toward the mass of players, and out of the group trotted a pale white horse and its rider.

The rider wore heavy black armor, his face obscured by a shiny silver Roman Calvary helmet, its crown rimmed in spikes, its face-plate frozen in a sinister sneer. One of his gauntlet hands was wrapped around the reins. The other arm sported a massive ornate crossbow attached at the wrist with a quiver of arrows on the side. A silver sword dangled from his belt. His armor also was covered with a hunter green robe, the gold ANYNONE symbol stitched in the center. Wicked green aura floated over all.

Guess this is the big boss, Snoops quipped.

"Who are you?" Kincaid shouted. "And what do you want with me?"

The man stood still, only breath replying from beneath his helmet.

They both stood there, frozen in the moment before battle, like two ships angled against each other in a bottle. Then the man reached toward his quiver.

Kincaid didn't miss a beat, instantly pulling up his battle spells and selecting *fireball.* His mana bar depleting as his staff belched a giant orange-yellow fireball that flew toward the man.

The fireball slammed into him and his horse, flames quickly engulfing them. The horse reared up and screamed, trying to run, but the rider dug his spurs into its flesh, forcing the horse down onto the ground as flames flickered around them. Eventually, the horse's scream faded, but the rider remained perched on the saddle, silent as a stone until the flames died down.

All that remained was cherry-red glowing armor, smoke streaming from gaps.

Kincaid stood there, shocked.

Then, miraculously, the man turned his head, his armor plates sparking against each other. He flung his leg over the saddle and dismounted, his horse crumbling to ash and bone behind him. The grass beneath his feet sizzled and burst into small flames as he stepped toward Kincaid, leaving behind blistering footprints. He grabbed the sword at his side and drew it, raising it over his head like a blacksmith from a forge, the blade glowing white hot. He reached up and grabbed the hilt with his other hand and swung the sword down forcefully.

A green crescent of energy flew out of the sword's tip and whistled just by Kincaid's head, tiny strands of hair falling. The energy flew into the rubble beyond and obliterated it.

Was that an energy slash—

Another green crescent whirled by, cutting part of his arm robe.

Kincaid raised his staff, ready to shoot another fireball, when the selection box flashed red. Mana bar empty again.

Fuck this.

"Snoops! We've gotta go!" he yelled, running away.

Snoops had just finished nut tapping one of the random Avatars who attacked him. He glanced over and nodded.

"Sorry, laddies," he said, curtsying to the remaining Avatars. "Duty calls."

Snoops shimmered simultaneously, growing larger and swinging his axe through three of them at once, instantly logging them out.

The other Avatars looked at him, shocked, stunned, and scared.

"WTF, that's so OP," one muttered as they turned tail and ran toward other battles, deciding to try their hands at easier foes.

Snoops caught up to Kincaid.

"What's up?" he said, Scottish accent abandoned.

More green crescents came flying toward them.

"Whoa!" Snoops exclaimed. "Are those freaking *energy slashes*? Do you know how long you need to play to have those?"

"Snoops, *focus*," Kincaid hissed.

"Roger, Roger. So what's the plan?"

"We need to get out of here fast. Transform into something that can get us airborne."

"You sure? You know my programming specifies only one Avatar shift per zone. Any more than that draws *other* attention."

"Yes, I know." Kincaid ducked another slash. "We have bigger problems than that. I authorize override, access code 0742!"

Snoops' eyes flashed blue.

Confirmed.

Snoops flickered and shifted into a massive, blue-scaled dragon with huge leathery wings, sharp talons, and fierce blue diamond eyes. He roared, scattering the horde around them. Kincaid scrambled up his leg, onto his back, settling awkwardly in-between a pair of spiky back spines.

Hold on, Snoops said, wings flapping and dirt flying as he used his massive hind legs to launch into the air.

A few crescents flew by, barely missing Snoops' outstretched wings.

With each beat, they picked up speed and altitude, the battle shrinking beneath them.

They flew for a while, as silent as the clouds surrounding them. Eventually, Snoops dipped below and they were above the edge of another large forest that stretched into the distance, a sea of unbroken green canopy.

A breeze picked up from the south, and the air seemed to warm for a moment before—

Flash!

The boom of thunder rang in his ears before Kincaid realized they were rapidly spiraling down toward the ground.

Looking over, he saw a giant flaming hole in one of Snoops' wings, its webbing fluttering feebly in the wind.

Snoops bellowed, furiously flailing his other wing, just managing to slightly pull out of their death spiral before his talons scraped against the earth, tearing huge chunks as they slid before hitting the ground.

The impact jolted Kincaid's entire body and slammed him right into one of Snoops' back spikes, his nose cracking, his staff flying from his hand into the forest.

"You okay?" Kincaid asked.

Snoops lifted his head from dirt and peered over at him.

I'm okay. Think we got hit with a lightning bolt.

Kincaid looked at the sky, dark clouds gathered directly above them. Static and lightning crackling within. *I don't think that's a normal storm.*

Another bolt flashed from the sky, striking the ground just to their left.

After the flash faded, they saw an army rapidly approaching from the distance. At its front was the armored man. Blue lightning danced around one of his gauntlets.

Snoops spotted him and growled then turned toward Kincaid and stared into his eyes.

Boss, you should high-tail it out of here. I'll hold them off for a bit and buy you some time.

"No, I'll stay and fight with you."

Snoops snorted, smoke curling from his nostrils.

First off, you lost your staff somewhere in that forest and second, they're after you, idiot. Besides, protecting you is fun!

Another lightning bolt struck the ground right in front of them. The hairs of Kincaid's neck rose from the impact.

Snoops reared up and shot a stream of bright orange and blue fire toward the army. The flames swirled like white-hot vengeance. The army burst from the flames seemingly unharmed.

A crescent flew through the flames and Snoops moved in front of Kincaid as it bit deeply into his hide. Red, steaming blood poured from the wound.

Snoops whipped his head in a large arc, spewing a stream of orange-blue flames on the ground, creating a massive wall of fire.

A crescent soared between the flames, cutting Snoops again. Several grunts poured through the momentary gap, their swords shining menacingly. Snoops curled up defensively, flicking his tail at some of the closest while moving his body back, pushing Kincaid closer to the forest's edge. The soldiers who dodged slashed eagerly down into Snoops' hide, their swords biting through his scales. Blood seeped from his wounds into the ground, creating a dark ruby mush. The flames burned lower and eventually, they were surrounded. Snoops eyed the army and dug his claws into the ground. His eyes grew brighter as he started to shimmer.

"Snoops, you can't!" Kincaid yelled.

Snoops snarled and shifted, transforming into a muscular giant with metal armor and a spiked club. He raised his club and roared.

Thunder boomed overhead.

Orange lightning spread through the clouds. With each echo, the thunder grew louder and lightning bolder. After every flash, large dark shadows spread over the bottom of the clouds, forming the shape of house cats. The thunder changed pitch until it sounded like hundreds of cats meowing through a sub-woofer.

The Schrodinger cats had arrived.

To preserve SCAPE's data resources and to prevent AIs from going rogue and not following protocol, SCAPE created AI monitors that placed the rogue AI into a Schrodinger box, forcing the AI into a quantum loop, exhausting their resources until they either logged out or disintegrated into data dust.

"Snoops, you need to stop!" Kincaid yelled.

Snoops swung his club through four grunts before he looked up at the sky and roared, shifting back into his dwarf form and yelled in his Scottish drawl, "I ain't scared of you pussies. If yer so fearsome, come and get me!"

The air sparkled and everything slowed. A tangerine box dropped from the sky and landed in front of Snoops, crushing several grunts underneath.

The armored man walked through the flames and looked at the box, then at Kincaid. He raised his hand and shot lightning toward Kincaid. A loud, annoyed cat meow echoed from the box and the lightning arced toward it, disappearing into orange nothingness. The man tried maneuvering around the box but a yellow warning sign appeared along with a dialogue prompt that read:

WARNING: Any interference with Schrodinger Monitors will result in instant force log-out and penalties will be applied to users' accounts.

The box creaked open, revealing pitch-black darkness inside. An arcade claw flew from within and snatched Snoops.

Snoops struggled, shifting forms, first back to the giant, then briefly, the dragon before back into the bloodhound from

Murder Alley, hoping to pry the claw loose. Yet, it remained firmly clasped. Snoops began to grow blue before bursting into light, trying to spin out of it. The claw glowed orange and threads of the blue light began streaking toward it.

Snoops' blue light faltered before fading, leaving Snoops now in the form of the teenage girl. Her neon hair dimmed. She looked back at Kincaid.

"Boss. It's time to go. Sparky over there can't do anything with this box here. Get away. Solve the mystery."

"But you'll—"

Snoops shook her head, eyes irradiating for a moment. "Don't worry about me."

The claw began to retract, pulling Snoops into the darkness beyond. The meows got louder as it did so.

Kincaid swallowed tears, turned, and ran into the forest beyond.

~~~

CHAPTER 10

The sound of cat meows echoed in Kincaid's head as he ran aimlessly through the forest.

He could still smell burnt flesh, hear twisted metal, and feel static in the air. His entire body buzzed with adrenaline. As he ran, his face was thwacked with tiny branches, and he stumbled over hidden roots, falling into thorn bushes and sharp rocks. The light in the forest dimmed the farther in he went.

He was in the middle of a clearing when he suddenly smelled gingerbread.

The odor was magnetic.

It took hold of him and before he knew it, he stood in front of a cottage. It looked like it was ripped straight from a storybook. Its siding was a quaint mismatch of different woods: oaks, elms, and maples. Two tiny circular glass windows with faded turquoise wooden shutters surrounded a deep red door with a brass star hanging crooked in the center. Strange plants, moss, and mushrooms grew in the window boxes. A thatched straw-covered roof lay overhead, broken up only by a slim brick chimney belching purple smoke. The property was surrounded by a wooden picket fence with purple-flowered ivy curling around the posts.

As Kincaid approached, a faint wisp of wind rattled the trees, and the wooden gate swung open noiselessly. He stumbled up the stone path, squirrels, chipmunks, and tiny gnomes fleeing from his presence. He approached the door, his fist raised toward the star to knock, when the brass handle turned and the door opened.

Warm golden light washed over him, along with the sweet smell of lavender, honey, and cloves.

When the light faded, he was somehow inside, sitting at a worn wooden table. A massive brick fireplace was to his right, a fire roaring underneath and a large black iron cauldron hanging over top.

A bony hand placed down a wooden bowl of steaming red soup.

Kincaid turned and saw a tiny old woman behind him. Her body hunched and draped in a midnight blue shawl with half-moons and stars that matched perfectly with her gray hair that was tied into a neat bun with a silver ruby-eyed owl hairpin. Her face was dominated by a huge beak nose with a dark brown mole on the right side. She looked at him with faint, lavender eyes, her head turning like an owl's. Her bio-data curled around in tiny infinity symbol loops.

"What? You don't like soup?" she exclaimed, her voice both gravelly and slightly high-pitched.

Kincaid shook his head.

"Then eat. That soup will help warm you up, full of lots of iron and protein, it is," she cackled.

He spooned some of it into his mouth. The soup tasted like cherries and blood, but it instantly warmed his body.

He peered at the woman's bio-data, then her movements. She was precise and limber for a woman of her age, yet there were slight variations. Almost imperceptible at first, but as he watched closer he realized they were intentional. Deliberate. Designed.

"Are you an AI?" he posed.

She nodded. "You wandered into the Grimm Forest."

The Grimm Forest was a section of FANTASCAPE where younger users could come and experience VRstories like *Hansel and Gretel, Rapunzel,* and other fairy tales. Due to the high demand, many of these stories were staffed with AIs rather than VRactors. This ensured consistency and customer satisfaction.

"I see," he said.

"How's the soup?" she asked.

"It's good."

"Excellent, I put a fresh batch of kids in there." She grinned.

"*What?*" Kincaid gasped, dropping the spoon and looking down at the soup, horrified.

"Relax," she chided, "I'm kidding."

Kincaid grabbed the bowl, twirling it to see if he saw anything in the soup, just to make sure. There was nothing. Of course, there wasn't. Even if there was, it'd just be bits of code and not actual children. He shook his head; he must be losing it.

The old woman looked at him, laughed, and walked over to the other side of the cottage toward a dark brown hickory cabinet. She reached into her collar and pulled out a gold key, its face a giant sun. She placed the key into the cabinet and twisted. The entire cabinet shook, as if shaking off a thousand other locks within. She tugged the doors open and reached inside, pulling out a stone mortar and pestle, a dark red leather book, and some glass vials filled with strange multi-colored powders.

"You look like you've been through a rough journey," she said. "Let me fix you a little potion for your pain. A full dose and you'll be feeling right as rain."

She began uncorking vials, dumping powders into the mortar, and grounding up others to add to it, sparks flying from the bottom of the pestle. She dumped all of them into a cloth square and bundled it up, tying it with a cord. She walked over to the cauldron and lifted the heavy lid with her bare hand and tossed the bundle into the liquid within. She grabbed a wooden spoon from the mantle and stirred. She stood there a few minutes before scooping out some of the liquid and pouring it into a clay coffee mug.

She placed the steaming mug in front of him. Kincaid looked at the contents suspiciously.

"Go on. Drink. I promise it's kid-free," she instructed.

He tilted the mug, sipping at first, then draining the entire mug in one go. It was delicious.

The liquid had barely left his throat when the room blurred slightly.

He grabbed the edge of the table, steadying himself.

"What's happening?" Kincaid wondered out loud.

The old woman looked over from the fireplace. "Oh, my potions have been known to have some hallucinogenic side-effects."

"Hallucinogenic?"

The wooden spoons got up and began to dance around the room on their tiny wooden spoon legs. The mug began to spin on its handle like a break dancer.

The woman's head grew four times its normal size, stretching like water being blown out of the end of a straw. Then it *popped* off, her entire head floating above her body before wandering toward him. The walls, floors, and plants all swaying to some unseen wind, their outlines shimmering with just a hint of rainbow effervescence.

"Just go with it," she said, her head spinning past his own.

A thud vibrated through the entire cabin. The room darkened and lengthened, stretching toward the sound. He followed the movement, taking in sharp, odd details along the way. The bright fuzz on a dish cloth, the faint odor of hanging herbs, the lazy smoke curls from the fireplace, the tiny strands of straw in the roof. The thud vibrated again. He looked and found the source. The door. Which seemed oddly funny to him. The thud echoed again, shaking the room. The door vibrated, splintered, then flew open. The room grew cold, and his dazed revelry took a dark turn.

In strode the rider, his black armor covered in blood and blue gore that seemed to pulse with the glimmer of its former lives. He approached Kincaid, his body growing in size and shifting too, transforming into the dark, green-suited man from Scarlett's tale, his Obscurio flickering between Guy Fawkes, Rorschach, and a blank dark sphere. He grabbed Kincaid, lifting him off the chair.

Kincaid stared into the Obscurio, the faint emerald gas and bio data swirling within, and on the outside, his reflection stretching, shifting. Dazed. Confused. Terrified.

"You might want to adjust the dosage a bit," he said, turning to the woman, who, still headless, continued to stir the cauldron, saying nothing.

Kincaid looked back into the blank, black sphere of the Obscurio. The man reached into his jacket and pulled out a dark crystal flask, black-blue liquid swirling inside.

"So this is the big bad death potion, huh? Gonna use it on me?" Kincaid said, laughing manically.

The man popped the crystal stopper off with his thumb. Then he slammed Kincaid down onto the table, hard. He grabbed the bottom of his jaw. He bent down closer to

Kincaid's face. In the reflection of the Obscurio, Kincaid saw the old woman's head pinned into the wall, sword sticking out of her middle, her lavender eyes cloudy.

Wait, what?

The room swirled and began to come into focus, pain crept around the edges, yet still felt distant. The man's hand squeezed around Kincaid's jaws and yanked his mouth open and poured the liquid into it.

It tasted cold and metallic.

Kincaid instantly turned to the side, coughing up some that got into his airway. It was only when the drops on the table began to smoke and curl up toward him threateningly he realized this was no longer a hallucination.

The man turned Kincaid's head back and poured more into his throat. Kincaid spit it up and moved to knock the vial away while gurgling, "No, stop—"

The man squeezed harder and shoved the vial into his mouth and tilted his head back once more. Kincaid tried grabbing the man's arms, but they were solid as rock. His clawing eventually became weaker, the edges around his vision turning black and red.

The last thing he saw was fluttering blue pixels, scattering like ash and butterflies.

~~

White hot pain lanced through Kincaid, like a thousand tasers screaming at once.

Why does death hurt so much? he thought as pain greeted him again.

He opened his eyes, expecting to see sadistic cherubs.

Instead, green light assaulted him. As it cleared, he realized he was floating in the middle of a black glass box, its edges lit with green light like something out of *Tron*.

His Avatar's reflection stared back at him, bio-data flicking in red and violet distress. Still in SCAPE.

From his reflection, he deduced his hands and ankles were bound with matching green handcuffs, made of code and light. He pulled against the cuffs, and the light flared, shooting pain through his body.

The dark glass rippled. A green line stretched out from the bottom edge, slowly forming the outline of a door. Once complete, the door turned the same green before disappearing and in walked the Green-Suited Man.

He stopped just in front of Kincaid, looking up at him with his mix of masks and faces. He snapped his fingers. Kincaid floated down and into a chair. Its twin appeared across from him with a narrow table in the middle. The man pulled the chair out, its legs scraping like nails across the glass, and sat down across from him. He placed his elbow on the table and leaned against his hand, bending closer toward Kincaid.

"Finally," he said with a digitized voice. "It's been a long road, but we've finally gotten a hold of you, Mr. Kincaid."

"How do you know my name?" Kincaid asked.

"We know almost everything about you, Dashiell Kincaid. Where you work, the types of cases you take, your clients, and even your spunky and quite unique AI."

"Don't you dare mention Snoops!" Kincaid roared, struggling to leap from the chair toward the man.

The man laughed. "I didn't do anything to it. You saw what happens to AIs who don't maintain control."

Kincaid gripped the edge of the table.

The man reached into his suit breast pocket and pulled out the crystal vial filled with the dark liquid code and placed it on the table in front of him. "I hear you've been looking for this. Well, here it is, why don't you take it?"

Kincaid spit on the man's Obscurio. It dripped down his shifting faces and onto the table.

The man reached up, touching it, seeming to marvel at the gesture. "My apologies, I realize this form might be a bit hostile to you. Allow me to change to a friendlier face..." He reached beneath his neck and pressed down. A hiss emanated. The Obsurcio faded to the black sphere. He removed it, the green suit fading away as he did so. Bio data trickled out and revealed the Avatar within.

Kincaid gasped. It was Dick Tracy.

Dick looked back at him, his golden hat and suit slightly crumpled. He smirked at Kincaid. "Told you I was close to finding my friend," he said.

What is he talking about? I've never met him until today. A dull ache began to pulse in Kincaid's head. He grimaced.

"Feeling alright?" Dick asked, his eyes alight with curiosity.

"I'm fine," he muttered, "but I don't know what you're talking about. We've never met before today."

Dick laughed. "Ah, you may be right; *we* may have never met. But like I said before, SCAPE is full of masquerades and subterfuge. You never know who you are interacting with at any given moment. In some sense, we're all just vivid echoes of consciousness, rendered in ever-changing digital flesh."

"Well, I'm not who you are looking for, I can promise you that."

"No, I promise you. You're *exactly* who we've been looking for," Dick said.

"Is that why you've chased me across SCAPE and the real world?"

"Partly, but that was only to motivate you to follow the breadcrumbs we laid out for you."

Breadcrumbs? Wait is he—?

"You killed Wendell Huntington and Alex Kyranos," Kincaid gasped.

Dick smiled, leaning forward. "Close. You're missing one piece. Let me show you."

Dick's bio-data flared, all protections removed. It flowed into Kincaid's mind. The data overwhelmed him at first, then he began recognizing patterns. Patterns he had seen before. But where? Then it dawned on him. In the Portal archives.

"You're... that's *Alex Kyranos'* Avatar. How, how did you...?"

"Don't insult yourself, Kincaid. You know Avatars can't be stolen that easily. That's the entire point of bio-data, right? You'd need massive amounts of DNA and months of reverse engineering the rig interface to replicate the micro-signatures from that DNA base. It's not something just anyone can do," Dick said.

The data did mention the logout after time of death but that still doesn't explain Miss A's...

"My wife is quite the actress, isn't she? She relished the opportunity to help revive a dying art. To my surprise, you took the bait rather easily. Guess you aren't as skeptical as you used to be."

"So you're really Alex Kyranos?"

"In here, I'm as much Alex Kyranos as you're Dashiell Kincaid. Believe what you want, but I know who I am. Can you say the same?" Alex said, his eyes blazing with serious certainty.

Of course, I know who I am. He's making no sense.

Yet, as he sat there in silence, the dull ache still blanketing his head, he saw flickers of something new appear in his reflection: doubt.

"Why did you fake your death?" he asked.

"Death allows for unlimited freedom, doesn't it? I needed certain people to believe I had perished so I could move as I wanted in the background, gathering my allies, setting up my pieces, and getting ready to make my final play," Alex said.

"And that play is using this code to kill billions of people?"

"This code does so much more than that. Think of it like a giant red pill, being force fed to billions."

Red pill, like from the Matrix? *Neo took that and...*

"You want to destroy SCAPE?" Kincaid exclaimed.

Alex sighed. "Not destroy it, necessarily. What I want to destroy are the masks and shadows on the wall and show everyone where the light is really shining from. SCAPE used to be about ultimate human connection, interaction, and freedom but it's been distorted and twisted into something else entirely."

"And that is?" Kincaid asked.

"Power. Control. A tonic to wash down greater sins. I want people to be free," Alex said.

"So you wake everybody up, what then? You think they'll thank you? Worship you? People's entire lives are built within and through SCAPE. You tear all that down, and then what? World peace? War? Are you ready to live with the consequences? More importantly, do you think the Portal will let you?" Kincaid's voice rose with every word.

"Once this code is in motion, they won't have a choice. The genie will have forever fled the bottle," Alex casually remarked. "Besides, there's already a war going on. One where you'll soon realize the unique role you have to play. As for the consequences, I've stared my sins in the face, and I am at peace with them. I know my reasons."

"And those reasons killed Wendell and Becky!" Kincaid yelled.

"And many, many others," Alex purred

Kincaid stared at Alex, flabbergasted by his casual admittance to multiple murders. He had to know.

"Why?"

"They were necessary sacrifices in this journey. This... war I'm fighting, *we're* fighting, it's bigger than one or two lives. Besides, you don't just throw a vaccine into the wild without testing it first. I didn't know if this really was the Terminal Code or just another fantasy. I've spent years chasing false hopes and empty dreams," Alex said.

"The Terminal Code?" Kincaid asked.

"Its creator had a clever sense of humor." Alex stood. "That's enough for now. I already told you where you need to go for answers. Like Theseus, you, Kincaid, must descend into the labyrinth and face your own Minotaur."

"Where is this labyrinth? How do I get there?" Kincaid asked.

Alex placed his Obscurio back on his head. The sphere contracted and hissed, his bio-data and yellow suit vanishing in an instant, replaced with sinister green. His digitized voice replied, "Easy, just drink that there. It's not the real Terminal Code, I promise. Think of it more like a chaser. It'll help the real shot go down easier. Once you wake up, you'll be exactly where you need to be."

Alex walked toward the glass, holding his hand outward. The green outline of the door appeared again and opened. He half walked out then turned back toward Kincaid, his Obscurio cycling between his thousand faces. For a brief moment, Kincaid saw a Greek porcelain theater mask within its face permanently frozen in anguish, then it vanished, hidden beneath a thousand more grins.

The door and Kincaid's restraints disappeared, leaving him free to roam. He got up and walked toward the glass, trying to see anything but his own confused reflection.

The vial loomed on the table. Questioning, threatening, and tantalizing.

Do I drink this? What is this labyrinth? Who is Alex fighting? What is this Terminal Code? Who created it and why? All those questions ran through his mind, raging for attention like children. Standing there, he realized nothing really had changed. The code still represented a flaw in the system, maybe even a threat to the world itself. And to eliminate it and keep SCAPE running, he had to understand it. He couldn't let this beautiful, perfect system succumb to the whims of a delusional madman.

He grabbed the vial, popped the top, and drank the liquid, descending into darkness once again.

~~~

CHAPTER 11

—

Kincaid awoke, draped in fog and silence.

He was lying on a cold, hard surface. He wrapped his knuckles against it, and a soft thud echoed all around him before returning to a hush.

A giggle pierced through the void.

"Hello?" he called out.

The giggle returned, this time to his right. He scrambled up and moved toward it.

The fog cleared slightly, and there stood the figure of a little girl. She turned to him, and Kincaid could see she had light auburn hair, a round-heart-shaped face, and light blue eyes.

It can't be?

"Snoops?" he said, holding his hand out.

The girl turned her head in a bird-like fashion, still staring at him. Her eyes seeming to hold the answer to an unasked question.

If she isn't Snoops, that means she must be....

"Rose?" he breathed.

She giggled again and ran into the fog.

"Wait!" he yelled, running after her. Her silhouette faded with each step he took.

The fog darkened again, swirling around him like phantoms before lifting as if blown away by a great wind.

In front of Kincaid stood a gray-green concrete wall. Its bottom was lit with a pale yellow light, creating a blurry line that stretched deep into the horizon. The wall was equally as tall and seemed to have no edge, with its terminus fading into fog.

This must be the labyrinth. But how do I get in?

Kincaid placed his hand against the wall. It met cold resistance at first, and then, like breaking the surface of an icy pond, it slipped through. Shocked, he pushed harder, and more of his arm disappeared into the wall. As it reached his shoulder, his fingertips warmed slightly, and he was sucked through.

He emerged onto a narrow path; another wall with its palely-lit bottom lay a few feet in front of him.

The air seemed warmer, as if full of some unseen energy or expectation.

Whispers crept up the walls. They grew in number and volume, surrounding him in a great din. Then quickly, they died down, replaced with a dull hum. Turning, Kincaid saw a swarm of fireflies, their bellies glowing yellow-green. The swarm pulsed and began rearranging itself, some fireflies glowing fiercely and others fading, forming outlines, angles, and forms. The forms shifted before settling on a giant sphinx, its body that of a lithe lioness, wings of a falcon, and head of a woman. Its cat-like eyes glowed with a pale yellow fire.

"What are you?" Kincaid asked.

"*You ask me who or what I am. Yet the answer is clear to all who look within,*" it said with a thunderous voice of a thousand whispers inside its head.

"*I am...*

Form and Feeling
memory and moment
shape and pattern
thread and needle
muscle and bone
ash and dust
First in line of your trials am I.
Two others await for you to try
Conquer both and revealed the truth shall be
But first, you must conquer me. Now, oh seeker, answer
now, my riddles three," it continued.

"Riddles, Really?" Kincaid asked.

The Sphinx grew in size, reared up, and roared at him, showing its long fangs.

Kincaid shuddered, his bio-data glowing in response. He was filled with a terrible sense of foreboding.

Guess I'll play along.

"Fine, hit me with the first riddle," he said.

The Sphinx sat and flicked its tail before uttering:

"You seek me in the questions that children often pose
yet other times you twist and bend me like a garden hose.
What am I?"

The questions that children pose. Hmm... twisting and bending... Could it be?

"Truth?" he asked.

The Sphinx shrank by a third, and it nodded and offered the second riddle:

"I dwell within the pool of your mirror's gaze
yet often I am unknowable, clothed in an endless haze.
What am I?" it said.

Dwell within the pool of your mirror's gaze, yet often unknowable? Hmm...

"Fear?"

This time, the Sphinx grew three times as large and roared before replying:

"Self is the answer you needed to say,

miss another riddle and will end your quest in this maze."

Kincaid nodded.

"I start as a whisper, a tiny little thing

but as time passes, I grow and fly away on billions of shouting wings.

What am I?" it said.

A whisper, flying. I wonder.

"Lies?"

The Sphinx shimmered and burst into a thousand shadows that swarmed around him before fleeing. In the middle of where it once stood, a round golden shield hovered.

"Passed this trial have you today.

Continue on for on this path the truth does lay.

Take this shield for your trials ahead,

protect you from enemies that lie in your stead," the Sphinx's voice echoed in his head.

Kincaid grabbed the shield and walked deeper into the labyrinth.

He hadn't gotten far when abruptly he stepped into water. An electric current pulsed through his body and some force pulled him forward. Suddenly, he was in the middle of a large pond. Its water was a murky blue with faint algae-green data swirling within. The same force pushed him deeper into the water like a giant hand slamming down. He barely caught a breath before he sank beneath the surface.

Struggling, he tried to swim upward but the weight of the shield dragged him deeper into the depths. The water grew darker as he approached the bottom, the data glowing like phantoms in the deep. His bio-data flared with distress, his lungs burning with effort, the edges of his vision turning white. He dropped the shield, and it fell like a stone to the bottom. He swam up to the surface, stroking the water furiously. He broke the top, gasping for air.

Treading the water, he inhaled again, taking deep breaths, unsure if he was about to be pushed deeper again.

He heard the gurgle of waterfalls and smelled lavender.

"Welcome, seeker," a husky female voice said.

Kincaid turned and saw a woman perched on a weathered rock that rose suddenly out of the water. Her body was arched back, arms loosely grasping the stone. One of her legs crossed in front of her, the other slowly stirring the water in lazy circles. She had long, straight red hair that stretched past her toes and disappeared into the water, twisting and tangling into the depths like eddies in a stream. Crabs, starfish, coral, and barnacles were dotted throughout it. Her skin glittered in the light like rainbow fish scales. Her lips were red and heavy, and full lashes shaded her bright green-gold eyes.

"Who are you?" Kincaid asked

She smiled. "I'm the nymph of this data pond and overseer of your next trial."

"So what is it?" he said.

"There is something lost at the bottom of this pond, which you must find and return to me. You have only twenty minutes to recover it"

"Twenty minutes? I can't hold my breath that long!"

She turned her head at him quizzically. "Strange thing, the human mind. You put it under water, and it thinks you will drown. Place it in the sky, and it will have you fall. But here... such things are arbitrary, simply wisps of data floating through space. Remember, seeker, there is no barrier you can't overcome. The only limits you face are those you place on yourself. Now, hurry, time is already ticking."

A green countdown clock appeared in the upper right-hand corner of his vision.

He dove. Swimming into the depths. A few minutes went by before his lungs began to burn. His vision once again tinged with white around the edges. He knew he had to open his mouth and let the water in, but some ancient primal survival instinct stood in his way. He clenched his fist.

There is no barrier I can't overcome.

He cleared his mind and opened his mouth, water rushing into his lungs.

He expected a sharp pain, and a soft descent into darkness. But to his surprise, nothing came. He inhaled and exhaled. Oxygen still flowed as it always had through the rig.

Amazing. I can't believe I never thought of this before.

He pushed deeper, the water becoming murkier. Soon, he spied a muddy bottom, strands of data tangling up from it like plants from the earth.

He swam just above it, looking out into the depths, searching for something, anything.

A gold light appeared in the distance like a beacon.

That must be it.

As he approached, he made out the shape of a large cliff, the gold light shining from the top of the underwater peak. Beyond the edge, the water darkened to a pitch black, no data emanated from it. As he drew closer, the light dimmed, and he could make out its source. A large rainbow pearl sat nestled in the middle of a large pink scallop shell. The pearl shone with fiery golden light like some godly beacon. The longer he looked at it, the more beautiful it became. He could understand why the nymph wanted it so much.

He swam toward it when something slimy and coarse wrapped around his ankle and threw him into the soft, thick mud. He pulled his face out with a great thuck and looked up with horror as a large, black shape floated up from beyond the cliff's edge. Blurry at first, it sharpened into the form of a giant gray Kraken. Its massive eight arms hung beneath its pluming mantle. Two larger tentacles stretched out, one of which was wrapped around Kincaid's ankle. He could feel the tiny serrations of the suction cups digging into his skin. Most frightening were the two large dish-sized eyes that stared at him with a sinister intelligence.

The Kraken raised its arms around the pearl, forming a moving, shifting cage. It plumed upward, its mantle increasing in size. The light of the pearl illuminated against its black, shiny sharp beak, which snapped threateningly. It wasn't going to give up the pearl easily.

Kincaid searched for something that might help him against this monster of the deep. He spied a human skeleton just beyond one of the Kraken's tentacles, its bony hand clasped around a rusted spear. He swam to it when the other tentacle slammed into him, pushing him deeper into the dirt.

I need to swim faster so I can get to that spear.

As soon as he thought it, he began moving through the water with ease, as if it were only air. He reached down and, with newfound strength, pried the other tentacle off his ankle. He zoomed around the other tentacle to the skeleton and snatched the rusty spear from its grip.

He swung the spear at one the Kraken's arms and sliced it clean in two. It shuddered, emitting a large bellowing bubble.

At the same time, a sharp pain split Kincaid's head in half. An image flashed through his head:

*A blond-haired boy nudging him in the arm, a PlaySta-
tion controller in his hand, a TV screen in front of both of
them, the screen reading GAME OVER...*

He shook his head, scattering the image just in time to
see the Kraken lunging after him with its tentacles. Kincaid
pivoted on a dime, easily avoiding the first, and jabbed with
the spear. He felt it enter, a tiny red cloud of blood leaking
from the wound confirming it.

His head flared again, another image flashed:

*A women with a heart-shaped face, brown eyes, and
auburn hair laughing and smiling at him...*

Shaking the image away, he noticed his head throbbing with
a dull ache. The Kraken moved to ensnare him with its other
tentacle, and he plunged the spear into the top of its mantle.

Another image appeared:

*A tiny girl with pale blue eyes running to him, her
arms outstretched...*

Kincaid gasped, the pain this time not limited to his head.
He felt a deep ache in his chest, as if his heart were about to
burst. The Kraken, uncaring, rose and surrounded him, its
black beak emerging fully from its deep gray folds. It lunged
closer, beak snapping. It caught Kincaid in the shoulder, tearing into his flesh, blood clouds curling slowly from the wound.
He yelled, sending a stream of bubbles to the surface.

The pain almost caused him to descend into the darkness.
But the image of the girl returned, her outstretched hands.
Somehow, he leaned into the pain, gritting his teeth. He
reared away from the beak, leaving a chunk of his shoulder
still in its clutches. More blood began to stream into the water,
turning his vision red.

He moved with an eerie swiftness around the Kraken
and thrust the spear straight into one of its eyes. The eye

bulged and burst like a balloon. The Kraken shook, a stream of bubbles coming from it. Kincaid tore the spear from the eye-socket, leaving a floating trail of blood and entrails. The Kraken jerked back, seeming to deflate, and it fell slowly into the deep. The last Kincaid saw of it was a single eye, burning with hatred.

He moved closer to the pearl, marveling at its brilliance. He tried reaching out to it, but pain shot from his shoulder to his toes. His one arm hung loosely, not responding to his commands.

Great.

Using the spear tip, he tore part of his shirt and fashioned a satchel. He placed the pearl into it and tied it using his one hand and his teeth. He kicked up to the surface and stroked with his one good arm. His progress was slow at first, but eventually, he began to rise to the shimmering golden light growing nearer.

"Welcome back, seeker," the nymph said as soon as he broke the surface.

She was bent over the edge of the rock, her face just inches from the water. Her reflection looked equal parts relieved and concerned.

Her lips pursed. "You're hurt."

He nodded, pain lancing through his body, already a large red cloud of his own blood surrounding him.

She reached into the water and yanked out a large clump of green seaweed. She tossed it to him. "Place that on the injury. It should help."

He reached out and wrapped his hands around the seaweed and placed it on his wound. A sharp cold pain shot through his body, followed by a warm tingling sensation. He lifted the seaweed from his shoulder and saw the wound had completely closed. He looked at the water and saw the blood was already clearing as well.

"Thank you," he said.

The nymph smiled.

"Down there I... saw things, felt things that feel strangely familiar... and pain, such pain," he said.

"Water is a funny thing," she stated, "always flowing, searching, changing. But water also remembers. It carries memories of those long past and forgotten truths. Perhaps you brushed up against some shore you once knew. "

He nodded and reached into his makeshift satchel and retrieved the pearl. Its glow seemed somewhat dimmer outside of the water. The nymph's eyes lit with greed. She snatched the pearl hungrily from his grasp, holding it out in front of her face. A slight tremor went up her arm, and a tiny tear leaked from the corner of her eye. The water stilled, turning as smooth as glass.

Kincaid cleared his throat, startling the nymph from her daze. He wondered how long he would've floated there had he not done anything.

"Thank you, seeker. This treasure means more to me than you know. Your task is complete, now all that remains is to conquer the beast who lies within the center. You will need all your courage, strength, and wits. Remember what you've learned here, and I see you've already found your reward,'" she said, motioning to the spear.

"This?" he asked.

She nodded and began to sing, the haunting sound echoing through the water up his arm to the spear. It vibrated, matching the pitch of her voice. The nymph gestured, telling him to place the spear in the water.

As he did, the vibrations created an eruption of foam and rainbow bubbles. Lavender, copper, and something nutty grazed his nose before the singing stopped as quickly as it came. The nymph seemed to fade, like a painting whose colors had washed out.

He raised the spear out of the water and was shocked. It now was a pure shining gold, its edge gleaming with new-found sharpness.

"Only this spear can slay the beast beyond. You must stab it in the heart, for any other injury will only insight its terrible and swift rage. Oh, and you'll need this as well," she said, reaching behind her and tossing him the shield.

As soon as he caught it, the fog returned, enveloping him completely. When it cleared, he was standing on the ground once more. The nymph and lake had vanished. Only a tiny starfish remained.

He grasped the spear and headed to the center of the labyrinth.

~~~

CHAPTER 12

The floors of the labyrinth sloped up, while the walls began to dip down and eventually disappear as it opened into a square. In the middle, a pyramid of stairs rose up to a platform, on top of which rested a golden altar. He had reached the center.

Kincaid stepped toward the altar and the fog thickened while pulsing with a sinister, eerie intention. Hot bursts of air tickled the back of his neck, making him pause.

Turning, he saw a large figure loomed over him. The fog cleared slightly, revealing twin curled horns, blazing red eyes, and deadly desires. The Minotaur had entered.

Hot air flared from its snarling pink snout, while sweat and gore-drenched black hair furled from its head down through the center of its muscular human male torso, blending into its bull legs. Scars crisscrossed its chest and hands. It held a massive stone club in its right hand. It opened its mouth and bellowed, swinging the club toward him.

Kincaid raised the shield just before impact, and they collided with a bell-like gong. The force shook his entire body and caused his arm to scream in fiery pain. Pain that didn't seem normal.

The edge of his vision blurred pink and tiny pinpricks of lights danced just out of view. A classic sign of Ritz inhalation. Intentionally or not, Mr. Qin had just raised the stakes. He would feel every blow, bruise, and break 150 percent more.

Kincaid exhaled and pushed the club off his shield and thrust the spear toward the Minotaur's ribcage. It bounced off one of the hard bones, leaving a shallow cut, red blood welling out of it. The Minotaur grunted and swung its other fist down toward his head. Kincaid dodged at the last moment, air whooshing from the force of the swing.

They circled each other, stepping like acrobats on a tightrope ready to spring.

Kincaid raised his spear and slammed it against his shield with a clang, yelling, "C'mon!"

The Minotaur dragged one of its hooves against the ground before charging. It swung its club upward, catching the edge of Kincaid's shield, twisting it up toward his face. The leather straps dug into Kincaid's arm, drawing blood. Kincaid staggered back, wildly swinging his spear, just catching the tip of the Minotaur's chin hair.

At the sight of Kincaid's blood, the Minotaur's eyes glowed, and it began a furious barrage of blows back and forth against the shield, tearing shards from it with each blow. All Kincaid could do was hold on. The Minotaur reared back and slammed the club into Kincaid's shield, sending him flying ten feet backward. He hit the ground with a loud crack. The shield flew from his grasp, now a twisted ruined thing. He coughed and blood flew from his mouth, his biodata blazing dangerously red.

Kincaid rolled over and felt something dig into his side. He reached down and pulled out... Dick's lighter.

What the—?

The Minotaur continued toward him. Kincaid scrambled up, squared himself, and threw the spear. It sailed... right past the Minotaur's head.

Fuck.

The Minotaur was just a few feet away, and he had no weapon, just the lighter. The nymph's voice repeated in his head: *the only limits are those you place on yourself.* Kincaid clenched the lighter so hard his knuckles went white.

Become a weapon.

The lighter warmed and he felt something shift. Looking down, he now held Alex's silver sword from FANTASCAPE.

He swung the blade toward the Minotaur, a fierce green crescent bursting from the tip. It arced through the air and slashed through the Minotaur's right wrist, severing it. The club hit the Minotaur in the head and tumbled to the floor. It screamed as blood spurted from the wound, painting its black hair a dark crimson red. It furiously grabbed the club with its other hand and ran toward him, eyes blazing.

Kincaid slashed again, another green arc hitting the Minotaur's upper haunch. The cut was shallower this time and only enraged the Minotaur more. It swung down with the club, and Kincaid met it with the blade. They collided with a loud crack, the force of the impact seeming to shake the entire labyrinth. The Minotaur snarled and pushed against the blade, splinters and sparks flying.

Kincaid's arms began to shake against the oppressive force. He somehow pushed the club off of the sword, ducked down, and used the trail of the blood from the Minotaur's bleeding wrist to slide beneath its legs, running for the spear that lay on the ground a few feet beyond them.

Grabbing it, Kincaid pivoted back toward the Minotaur, which barreled toward him.

He swung the sword in a wide arc parallel to the ground, the crescent rocketing toward the Minotaur's legs. Just before impact, it crouched and leapt into the air. The slash passed harmlessly beneath. The Minotaur soared through the air with its club reared back, high overhead, its chest thrust out and heaving.

Kincaid gripped the spear tightly. He squared his stance, aimed, and threw the spear again. This time, his aim was true. It struck the Minotaur straight in the chest.

The Minotaur gasped at the impact, then snorted, flexing its thick chest muscles, stopping the spear only a few inches into its body. It grinned and continued its advance.

Kincaid roared and sprinted toward the Minotaur. He focused on the club over its head. He leapt up and swung the sword toward the spear as the Minotaur swung the club toward his head. The air shimmered, and the weapons changed places.

The sword sliced through Kincaid's chest straight to the bone. Red-hot pain spread. Kincaid clenched his jaw and let the gravity, weight, and momentum guide the club in his hand straight onto the end of the spear, like a hammer. The spear remained stubbornly in place for a moment before sinking deeper into flesh. Great rivulets of blood poured from the wound.

The Minotaur's eyes bulged, its neck muscles twitching. It let out a great and terrible yell before falling to the ground with a massive thud. Its tongue hung loosely from the side of its mouth, eyes rolled back in its head showing only permanent white. A giant puddle of blood spread from the corpse.

Kincaid fell to his knees, his own blood mixing into the puddle. Each breath shot waves of pain through his shaking body. His vision swam, blurry and spot-filled darkness flickering on the edges like a hungry flame. The sword shimmered and reverted to the lighter, now slightly dented. A great shudder spread through the labyrinth, clearing the fog. The walls shrank to only twelve feet high. He could see the entire maze. A pale beam of sunlight shot down from above, hitting the golden altar, painting everything in a warm glow.

Kincaid bent down to grab the lighter when another great shudder erupted, ending with a giant crashing sound, as if ancient stone walls had come crumbling down.

Alex's voice entered his head: "Kincaid, you must hurry to the altar. Now you've beaten the Minotaur, they've broken the encryption."

"Who's they? What encryption?" he gasped.

"You'll know soon enough. Our forces can hold them off for a bit, but it's crucial you get to the altar *now!*" Alex commanded.

A wall in the distance exploded, bursting into pieces of dust and bits. When they settled, a horde of red, faceless Avatars swarmed in.

The lighter twinkled and began to spin, faster and faster, until Kincaid heard a rip and a giant portal appeared. Out of the portal streamed legions of green-outlined Avatars, each with a gold ANYNONE symbol in the middle of their chests. They all held giant, menacing-looking shotguns. They fanned out in formation, surrounding him and blocking his view of the incoming forces.

"Go!" Alex shouted.

Kincaid pulled himself off the ground. His vision swam with spots and stars. Blood trickled from the wound. His bio-data flashed, fighting to suppress the signals to his brain in the real world. He somehow made his way to the beginning of the stairs and gingerly climbed his way up, wondering if his legs would fail and if he would tumble down and out of SCAPE, back to a sweat-filled rig.

Shotgun barks in the distance broke his daze. The opposing forces had begun their battle. He grabbed the edge of the altar and pulled himself up, looking upon the golden masterpiece.

The base of the altar was a small-scale replica of the Ark of the Covenant. Yet, as he gazed at the sides of the base, the panels seemed familiar. An old PlayStation controller, a rooftop Buddha garden, and a small ring box.

Kincaid placed his hand onto the altar, and a deep electric pulse shot through his entire body. The altar vibrated for a moment before sliding away, revealing a deep pit. His legs buckled, and he fell forward, into cool darkness below.

~~

When the darkness lifted, Kincaid was surrounded in a mix of light, shadow, and moisture.

Kincaid felt a strange sense of displacement. He was above and below. Here and there. In and out. Up and down. Heavy and weightless, all at once.

The shadows shifted, and the geometric twists and turns of the maze appeared reflected above and below him. The green and red Avatar armies, reduced to dots, clashed like fireflies on a summer's eve. Portions of the maze disappeared in great clouds of data, dust, and debris.

A blue glimmer caught his eye. A data cord trickled from somewhere above and below into his Avatar. Beyond that, it trailed into his real body, suspended in the rig. Seeing both bodies made Kincaid realize he felt apart from both, a cloud of consciousness, un-tethered.

A download bar appeared, its green letters reading:

dk_root.mm downloading....Progress: 0%

Finally, a voice echoed inside his consciousness.

Who's there?

An old friend, one who's very excited to be with you again.

Again? What the hell are you talking about?

I'm talking about that feeling in the pit of your stomach, the back of your throat, the tremor in your heart, the faltering in your step. The fear that's been forming in your mind ever since you took this case.

Bullshit.

More sections of the maze burst into dust. The red army split into two flanks. They moved to surround a portion of the green army in a pincer formation. Kincaid tried yelling down to warn them, but his voice was silent, only his thoughts screamed. The red army sprang their maneuver, obliterating that portion into a cloud of data dust.

Progress: 20%

Lie to me all you want, but I know the truth: you're beginning to question all you know and ever knew.

How?

Haven't you realized yet? Haven't you already questioned it, the black hole in your mind, the emptiness, the pain?

That can't be possible.

Did the labyrinth teach you nothing? Limits don't exist in SCAPE, only infinite possibilities.

So you're... me?

The green army was in trouble. The majority of the forces pushed back into a defensive position around the center of the maze. The red army circled like a pack of wolves, swarming, attacking, and retreating. They did this repeatedly, testing for weak portions in the line, pulling off weaker strays and swiftly putting them out of their misery. The lines dwindled.

Progress: 50%

Yes, a version of you preserved in code.

But why would I do that?

Necessity breeds strange bedfellows. Besides, you should know how fickle the mind can be.

I still don't understand.

His inner voice was silent for a moment.

Behold.

Space shimmered. New data strings slowly emerged out of his bodies. They floated into the maze toward the dueling armies. The strings stopped just above them for a moment before going through both and into a gray area beyond, filled with shadow and mist.

The mist swirled before two larger shadowy figures appeared within. Each held a set of strings. Both pulled. His bodies jerked in multiple directions. The figures looked at each other and began pulling at their set harder, his bodies pulled back and forth. Soon, tiny cracks began to appear, which grew larger with each tug. Shards of his bodies broke off in chunks, fading into data dust. The figures tightened their grip around the strings, and both pulled with all their strength. His bodies, unable to bear it any longer ripped in two. A great blue light bursting from within. When the light faded, a glowing glass vial rested in-between his two halves, its contents a dark black liquid full of code.

What is this?

A vision of the truth. Quite the Pinocchio, aren't you?

Progress: 90%

That's the Terminal Code, wasn't it...? But why was it inside of me/us?

We and it are linked together... bound by a fate yet to be determined. Though it seems for not much longer.

The lines of the green army broke. The red army swarmed in and cut off sections. Now separated, portions of the green army began to fall faster. The red army pushed against the last small circle line of the green. The green line pushed back a few, but slowly they, too, began to fall. The altar shook. The world flickered, growing brighter then darker. The only main source of light came from the download bar above.

How do we stop them?

Sometimes the only way forward is to look backward. Echoes of the past are yelled endlessly into the future. Whether or not we hear them, is unknown.

Progress: 100%... Initializing.

Pain shot through his head as he descended into code and memory.

~~~

CHAPTER 13

———

Our love for order/rules started early... his inner voice whispered.

The memory faded into place like *Tetris*, chunks of code at a time. They fluttered, resolving themselves into three dimensions then coming in and out of focus before settling into perfect virtual definition.

Snow fell outside of a French window, contrasting against the warm interior of a small cape cod house. A tiny fire smoldered in the fireplace. A frayed Kashan burgundy rug lay over worn pine floors. A coffee table came into view, its top covered with half-empty bags of Cheetos, Doritos, an empty container of Oreos, and a half-drunk, two-liter bottle of Mountain Dew perched straight in the middle. Two glasses filled with the bright green liquid rested on coasters just beyond that, a last ditch attempt at decorum. A tiny TV hung on the opposite wall, cords snaking out of the back down to a PlayStation 4, lounging on its original worn box as a stand.

A gray couch came into view, two boys plopped on it.

The first seemed familiar, as if Kincaid had seen him many times before but only just remembered. The boy looked up for a moment, meeting his eyes. They matched his own. Realization dawned.

That's me.

The other had long blond hair that looked like it hadn't seen a comb in weeks. Pimples dotted his greasy skin. Thick, black-framed glasses covered brown eyes that were narrowed in concentration. He wore a faded *Teenage Mutant Ninja Turtle* t-shirt covered in bleach stains, his legs clothed in off-brand black sweatpants. The only newer-looking item was his shoes, a pair of pristine white Air Jordans. He moved his limbs awkwardly, having the slightly stretched-out look of a boy just beginning his march into adolescence. His hands clutched the controller, skinny fingers furiously flying from the joystick to the thumb pad, leaving a trail of Cheeto dust in their wake. A neck vein bulged as he strained toward the TV in the corner.

The TV flashed, colors and pixels resolving into a pair of two fighters. One in yellow, the other blue. Scorpion and Raiden from *Mortal Kombat.* The boys fought through their characters, each getting a pair of combo hits on the other before Scorpion knocked Raiden's health bar down to nothing. "Finish him!" a deep voice echoed from the TV.

Scorpion spun, plunging his arm into Raiden's chest, ripping out his heart and crushing it, blood splattering the screen, the word *Fatality* appearing within it.

"Ha, got you!," the blond boy squealed, his voice cracking.

"Alex, that last move was fucking cheap and you know it," the younger Kincaid retorted.

Alex rolled his eyes. "Please, just because you can't improvise on the fly doesn't mean I have to pull my punches."

"Bet you can't dodge this one," Kincaid roared as he playfully punched Alex in the shoulder.

Alex winced on impact, rubbing it quickly. The boys' strength was starting to change. Soon, their fights would have lingering consequences.

Alex sighed. "As much as I *love* kicking your ass, you sure we can't do something else? Maybe look at some of your grandpa's old *Dick Tracy* comics in your dad's study?"

"Those comics are lame and boring. Why the hell are you so obsessed with them?" Kincaid asked.

Alex nudged him in the shoulder. "They aren't lame, they're *classics*. The characters, the dialogue, the mystery! It'd be amazing to create something like that one day," Alex answered.

"N-E-R-D alert," Kincaid said, making beeping sounds.

"Takes one to know one, Dash," Alex retorted.

"I hate that nickname, and you know it," Kincaid seethed.

"People don't get to choose their nicknames, they're bequeathed on them," Alex said, waving his arms, "like magical swords, busty-princesses, mysterious quests!"

"There goes the alert again. Set it off one more time and you'll keep girls away till you're forty!" Kincaid replied.

"And you're so mature the ladies are just crawling over themselves to get a piece of the incredibly sexy *Kincaid*. What lame-ass prefers to be called by their last name, anyway?" Alex questioned.

"Many people have been called by their last names throughout history. Gandhi, Hemingway, Picasso, Warhol, Obama, and so on. It's classy. You should try it, I'm sure the girls would go crazy over the mysterious *Kyranos*. Then again, maybe not, sounds like some fancy Ibiza-STD after all." Kincaid explained.

Alex flicked him in the side of the head. "Watch it, Mr. Classy, or next time the almighty Kyranos might not be so merciful," Alex replied in a deep mocking voice.

"Mr. Classy will take you on, double or nothing. If I win, we keep playing. If you win, we can go look at as many stupid comics as you want."

Alex grinned. "Oh, it's on like Donkey-Kong, I'll *totally* kick your ass again, unless you're tired of sucking."

"Funny. Your mom just mentioned that to me last night," he retorted, clicking onto to the main menu and selecting Sub-Zero.

Alex's eyebrows raised. "Really? Going for the classic matchup? You *must* be desperate."

He was about to respond when they were interrupted by the slam of the kitchen door, the TV shaking on the wall.

"What do you mean it's all gone?" a female voice yelled. The door opened as Kincaid's mother Judy blurred through into the living room, her curly red hair matching the current color of her face. She wore a pearl necklace, a slightly faded blue sweater and gray yoga pants.

"I called the bank, and they said the account was drained. There were a bunch of charges from a Vegas hotel," a male voice replied, following her. Kincaid's father, Edward, entered the room behind Judy sheepishly, wearing a checkered sweater vest, a button-down, slacks and thin wire-frame glasses.

"Well, did you tell them you didn't make those charges?" Judy asked, coming back into the middle of the door frame, her hands latched onto her hips.

Edward came up to Judy, placing his hand on her arm; his wedding band gleaming from the fire's glow.

"I did but..."

"But what, Edward?" Judy inquired, turning back toward him, searching his face with her pale-blue eyes.

"I called the other banks, and the credit card companies. Everything is either gone or maxed out. *Everything,*" Edward said, looking down, his voice shaking.

"How can that be?" Judy asked with all the incredulousness a Midwestern girl can muster.

Edward cleared his throat. "They said it looks like a classic case of identity fraud. But they said we have to provide proof."

Judy huffed, dragging Edward by his collar into the living room past the boys to an antique hutch in the corner. She flung open the cover like a woman possessed and began digging through files. Her hands sifted through so fast papers scattered like pigeons on a sidewalk, flying in every direction.

Edward stood behind her hovering. "Honey, I don't really think that's necessary."

Judy flicked away his request with a glance. As she dug through the papers, his glasses fogged up in anticipation or perhaps hope.

Then Judy stopped suddenly, her breath catching in her throat. Edward reached toward her, concern painted on his face. "Honey, are you alright?"

She recoiled from his touch, staggering away a few steps, her hand resting on the edge of the hutch, steadying herself. She turned toward Edward, a blue piece of paper clutched in her hand.

At first, Kincaid didn't hear his mother's words. They escaped from her as softly as feathers from a pillow. It was only after his father asked again he heard.

"Edward, what is this?" She held up a blue paper to his face. It looked like a receipt.

Edward's face turned ghost-white. "I—" he stammered.

"It's an ATM withdrawal receipt from Caesar's Palace in Vegas," Judy seethed. "What in god's name were you doing gambling in Vegas? Is *this* why all of our accounts are drained?"

"No, I swear... most of the charges are fraudulent," Edward whispered.

"*Most?*" Judy inched closer to her husband, holding the receipt closer to his face as if its proximity would reveal answers.

"It's true," Edward replied. "Some colleagues and I drove up from Phoenix after the Engineers conference. We went to the casino, and I lost some money..."

"*Some* money?" Judy turned back to the hutch, grabbing a credit card statement. "Then why does it say you charged two nights at Caesar's? There's also other small charges on here."

Judy leaned in closer to the paper. "Looks like there's an eighty-dollar charge on Wednesday and a $150 charge on Thursday. What, pray tell, were you spending all of that money on? Steak dinner for you and the boys?"

"You know Don and Jerry don't eat meat," Edward said.

Judy rolled her eyes and moved right next to her husband's face. "That's not what I meant, Edward, and you know it."

Judy poked her index finger into his round stomach. "What," *poke*, "were you," *poke*, "doing?" she demanded, before stopping on the last poke, a sudden realization dawning on her face. "*Who* were you with?"

Kincaid froze. He didn't believe what his mother had just said. His father would never do something like that. He loved his wife and son dearly. Surely, he couldn't do something that cruel and selfish?

Edward went so white he was practically translucent. He licked his lips, "Judy, I..."

Whatever Judy saw reflected in Edward's eyes forever altered Kincaid's life. She turned away from Edward, a tear streaming down her cheek, and she stormed out of the room. Edward stood there for a moment; a statue rendered in waxy guilt.

"Dad?" Kincaid said.

Edward turned toward his son and his friend, realizing for the first time they had witnessed the whole scene. He motioned toward his son, looking like he was going to speak. But whatever the words were in that moment drifted away as he slowly dropped his hand and walked out of the house. The front door closed quietly.

"Yo, dude... that was um, rough," Alex said, reaching over to him, squeezing his shoulder.

Kincaid stared ahead at the TV screen, fighting back tears.

Alex shook him gently, breaking his daze. "Um... I think I'm going to go," he said, creeping toward the door.

"Can you... stay? I can just watch you play *Metal Gear Solid* or something? I need to zone out," Kincaid asked.

"Sure, man."

Alex went over to the TV and switched games.

Soon, Kincaid was watching Snake scale over broken walls and fight off armies of enemies. Watching, he realized something. Snake only fought monsters, solved puzzles, and saved the day because that's what he was programmed to do. There was a kind of beautiful symmetry in that. Virtual games had programmed rules. A kind of boundary. Even with cheat codes, there were limits to the actions a character could take. Nothing unexpected ever happened, unless it was purposefully put there. No sudden discoveries, no hidden agendas, just plain and simple outcomes.

As Kincaid stood there, staring down at his younger self, other memories came flooding back.

His dad later fell victim to a phishing scam. His parents' credit cards and banking account info all appeared on the dark web, for sale to the highest bidder. Worse than the financial ruin was the infidelity. A double whammy shook the foundations of trust in his parents' marriage, breaking it completely. His once stable home became chaotic. His mother became erratic, losing herself in bottles of pills and wine. If not for Alex and his family, Kincaid might have ended up on the streets or worse.

The memory dimmed, fading and shifting...

~~

A conference room came into view.

An older version of himself sat in front of a long, glass table. He wore an ill-fitting blazer over a faded Batman t-shirt, with too-small jeans. A battered Mac Book Pro covered in brewery stickers sat in front of him. Outside of the window, the bay of San Francisco glittered in the sunlight.

Next to him was Alex. Older also, he wore a navy-blue suit, white shirt, and a thin, blue tie. His acne had cleared up, his skin tan, blond hair combed back, glasses gone. His leg was shaking, hitting the underside of the table with a dull thud. In front of him was a thick, black leather folder with a blue pen on top.

The doors opened and a group of suits walked in. They fanned out across the other side of the table. Two sat down at the table in front of them. A large Asian man, wearing a tight black suit that showed off his muscles and a woman in a gray pant suit.

The woman's hair was auburn-colored and curled. She glanced at him, her eyes golden brown like a sunrise on freshly fallen autumn leaves. She smoothed out her skirt, cleared her voice, and said, "Welcome to SCAPE headquarters, gentlemen. My name is Emily Cohen and this is my colleague,

Ito-san. We'll be the primary negotiators and liaisons for your licensing agreement."

Emily and Ito held out their hands. Alex shook Ito's hand then Emily's. He marveled at the smoothness of her skin and picked up the faint hint of lavender perfume.

"Why don't you tell me some more about your company, Apex, was it?" Emily suggested.

"Apex Entertainment," Alex replied, clearing his throat, "As you know, we're the creators of *Precipice*, a multi-player shooter/puzzle game. *PCMag* named it its top game in 2023. To date, we've sold five million copies and are projected to hit ten million by year's end."

"Quite the haul, and who's on your team?" Ito asked.

"Primarily us," Alex replied. "I handled the story and business end, while Kincaid does back and front-end design, with help from a few student developers."

"Yes, we started making games in our dorm room at Cal Tech for fun," Kincaid added. "I double-majored in AI and Computer Science while Alex majored in Business with an English minor."

"Impressive," Emily remarked, staring at him. "Personally, I love *Precipice*, but I always get stuck on level seven. Those damn windmills."

Kincaid blushed. "Level seven can be tough, but it's easy once you know the trick." He gulped and added, "Perhaps I could show you sometime?"

Emily blinked a few times, her face flushing.

Alex kicked him under the table, shooting him a look. "Let's get down to business, shall we?"

"Let's," Ito agreed. "You are proposing a four-game contract with a 30 percent revenue split while we handle marketing and distribution."

"Yes," Alex insisted, "we actually have a demo of a new game we're working on that we would like to start with." He turned to Kincaid.

Kincaid opened his computer, pulling up the new game demo when a tap on the door interrupted them.

"Takahashi-senpai?" Ito stammered, rising to his feet and bowing. Emily and the others in the room followed suit.

Hiroshi Takahashi, inventor of SCAPE, casually walked through the door, wearing a light white cotton kimono shirt, black fitted pants, and sandals. His face was slightly lined, and he had a large white streak in the middle of his otherwise jet-black hair, making him look badger-like. His eyes, a steel gray, shone with joyful intelligence.

He waited for everyone to straighten from their bow before saying, "I was wondering if I could take Kincaid-san here for a walk through the garden. It's such a beautiful day after all, not a cloud or wisp of fog in sight!"

"Sir," Emily pleaded, "we're in the middle of negotiations. I don't—"

Takahashi held up a hand, cutting her off. "I think Kyranos-san can handle the finer details, yes?" Takahashi gestured, looking at Alex, steel-gray eyes shining. Alex tugged his collar, gulped, and nodded. How could he refuse? Takahashi turned toward Kincaid.

Sweat began dripping down Kincaid's brow. He looked at Alex, who glared back at him as if mentally shouting, "Do not fuck this deal up by getting cold feet and refusing to go on a walk with your idol, you idiot!"

Holy Shit. Takahashi wants to meet with me?

Kincaid clumsily got up from the table and followed Takahashi out of the room. They walked down a narrow hallway through a doorway into the garden beyond. A cobblestone path meandered through a tiny tea garden complete with stone Buddhas, bonsai trees, and a stream that ran through it. Flowers and moss dotted throughout. Beyond, the city skyline beckoned, seeming close, yet so far away at the same time.

"Beautiful, isn't it?" Takahashi said.

"Yes," Kincaid replied.

"Did you know we plan to move our headquarters to New York City?" he asked. "The local government there has been very generous with its tax incentives. We will anchor a new downtown plaza, revitalizing the city once more. You should see the plans for the building, I imagine its gardens will one day be even more spectacular than this."

Takahashi clasped his hands behind his back and moved down the path, gesturing for Kincaid to follow.

They walked in silence, Kincaid too nervous to say anything.

"What do you think of Emily-san?" Takahashi blurted, peering at him, a deviant grin on his face.

"What?" Kincaid gasped, then blushed. "I think she's great... very, um, professional."

Hiroshi nodded, his eyes twinkling. "Yes, she's very good at her job. Though, I worry she spends too much time on me. She should think of herself now and again," Takahashi mourned.

Kincaid mumbled something incomprehensible in reply.

Takahashi, as if sensing his pain, changed the subject and remarked, "I've played *Precipice* many times. It's a very-well designed game. It draws you in but doesn't overwhelm you. The progression in the levels feels so natural. So balanced."

"Thank you, Mr. Takahashi. That... means the world to me," Kincaid breathed, his eyes welling.

Takahashi paused, bending closer toward him.

"Please, call me Hiroshi," he insisted. "We're fellow designers after all. I was in your shoes once, a young man no one took seriously trying to make my mark on the world."

"I'd say you made an impact," Kincaid retorted.

Hiroshi chuckled. "Yes, I suppose so. But it all started from a love for games. I wanted to make a new way people could experience, play, and explore. What's the one thing you love the most about games, Kincaid-san?" Hiroshi asked.

Kincaid thought for a moment. "When I was younger, I looked to games for escape. Entering into worlds, becoming characters I never could be in real life, doing impossible, even scary things I'd never do myself. But as I've grown older and things have happened, I've come to appreciate the order behind the games. As much as they might delight and surprise the player, the code itself always plays by the rules."

"Interesting, you seem to suggest code is without human flaws. Yet, the way you code, design, and construct is so full of joy and freedom. Where else does that come from if not yourself?" Hiroshi remarked.

Kincaid stood there, considering it. He had never looked at it that way before.

"Relax," Hiroshi chuckled, breaking him out of his daze. "No need to redefine yourself in one conversation. All I'm really saying is I'm jealous of it. It's a freedom I'm afraid I've lost in my age."

"I don't think you've lost anything," Kincaid said.

Hiroshi shook his head. "Please don't flatter me; the world I've built is beautiful, wondrous even. But every artist knows when their creation is missing something. I've built SCAPE from nothing. It took *years*, so much... *sacrifice*. Yet, still it feels incomplete, I can feel it yearning for something. A sense of *Kaizen* perhaps. I think you can help bring that to SCAPE," Hiroshi commented.

"Me?" Kincaid gasped.

They had come to a small waterfall that trickled from the top of the roof down into a small pond, which fed the stream. Dragonflies buzzed around a few lily pads, a frog looked out at both of them with green eyes, koi fish circled beneath trying to catch bubbles. A stone bench rested just in front of the water's edge. Hiroshi walked over to it, sat down, and patted the empty space next to him.

Kincaid rushed to join him. Hiroshi smirked and continued, "I want SCAPE to be everything for anyone. A blank canvas they can mold and shape however they choose, unencumbered by limits. But I'm not blind either. The world is constantly changing, shifting. Empires rise and fall, companies grow and evolve. Power is consolidated, broken, or taken. Someday, they will come for it."

"Come for what?" Kincaid asked.

"Freedom. Control. Influence. It goes by many names. When the minds of humanity focus on something so intently, some people feel lost, left out. Like petulant children, they reach out, screaming and demanding to be heard. SCAPE is a beacon of humanity, one of our crowning achievements. Beacons can empower and they can blind."

"What do you mean?"

"As much money as I have, power I've accumulated, competition I've destroyed or bought, one day I'll be gone and my creation will be left alone, at the mercy of an often cruel and uncaring world. My greatest hope is it can evolve organically with its users but its original purpose to inspire and delight isn't lost," Hiroshi confessed.

"Isn't that a bit contradictory?" Kincaid commented, "Don't our creations grow beyond us? Take *Precipice* for example. I built it with an express purpose and desire, but what it means to me versus those who play it are two very different things. You can't hope to force your beliefs of what SCAPE is and how people interact with it onto others."

"This is precisely why I wanted to meet with you," Hiroshi declared, patting Kincaid's hand. "When you work on something as long as I have, you become blind to its faults. Sometimes you need a different perspective. As you said, I can't and wouldn't force my beliefs of what SCAPE is and means onto others. But others will try. This is why I need you."

"Need me for what?" Kincaid asked.

"I need you to help me build something. Call it a failsafe of sorts, something I don't know about, something I can't stop, something that can prevent SCAPE from being distorted into something other than a beautiful canvas. A bitter pill of truth, a deadly poison, a Terminal Code," Hiroshi declared.

"A Terminal Code? What do you mean?"

Hiroshi looked off in the distance. For a moment, he seemed to age far beyond his years.

"Something that can destroy SCAPE itself, if needed," Hiroshi proclaimed.

"Destroy it? Are you crazy?" Kincaid exclaimed, leaping off the bench "Why would you want me to build something that could destroy your legacy, your livelihood, the livelihood for your children, grandchildren, your employees?"

"I've made enough money to secure bright futures for generations of my descendants, and my employees will be taken care of. But none of that will matter if SCAPE is used to divide, exploit, and tear apart the world," Hiroshi forewarned.

"Do you really think that'll happen?" Kincaid challenged.

"Yes, I do. So the only question that remains is will you help me, Kincaid-san?"

"I can't. I can't destroy something so beautiful, so amazing," Kincaid replied, exasperated.

"That's exactly why I want you to," Hiroshi said, looking deeply into Kincaid's eyes. "You'll have every resource at your disposal and you can build whatever other games and projects you'd like. It won't be easy, you'll be spending a lot of time here. But I think you'll find hard work and good intentions can lead to something amazing."

Kincaid's mind flashed to Emily, then to Alex. Opportunities like this, especially two at once, didn't present themselves often. He'd be a fool to turn down either and, like Hiroshi said, he had no idea where each might end up. He gripped the edge of the bench, steeling himself before turning to Hiroshi and said, "I'll do it."

Hiroshi stood up and bowed deeply. "Thank you, Kincaid-san. I look forward to working with you."

~~~

CHAPTER 14

—

The scene shifted, fading into a cozy New York city apartment. Now, an even slightly older version of himself sat hunched in front of a large holographic computer screen. The glow of the screen shone off of his wedding ring.

A TV droned on in the background.

Emily walked into the room. She wore yoga pants and a sports bra with a loose sweatshirt over top. Her hair was pulled back into a ponytail. Her face glowed. She put her hands over his eyes, her wedding ring sparkling, and spoke gently into Kincaid's ear.

"Honey, stop working and come feel her; she's kicking," she requested

Kincaid pulled her hands off of his eyes and looked at her incredulously. "Are you sure?" He gently swept her off her feet and twirled with her onto the couch. "The doctor said she wouldn't be moving for another week or two."

"Gentle," she chided, hitting him lightly on the shoulder. "Feel," she said, moving his hand confidently over her stomach.

Kincaid stood there for a moment, feeling nothing but the steadiness of her breathing, the pulse of her heart. Then, like a tiny flutter of butterfly wings, he felt movement. The early stirrings of life.

"I felt her," he gasped, his eyes brimming.

"You did?" Emily exclaimed, her eyes instantly matching his own.

Kincaid nodded, kissing her neck five times until she giggled.

"Stop," she pleaded, attempting to pull away while he held her tighter, not wanting to let go of the moment.

Kincaid thought back to the time they first met, five years ago. How beautiful she looked across the table. Looking at her, glowing in the height of her pregnancy, he realized she looked even more beautiful now.

Emily looked at him lost in thought and said, "What are you thinking about?"

"I was thinking about when we first met, and our slow dance to dating," he replied slowly, tracing his fingers up her arm. "Remember how our meetings went from monthly, to weekly, to daily? We were so cautious at first... and then boom, fireworks. At one point, I felt bad for whomever sat on that office couch of yours."

Emily slapped his arm. "Dashiell!" she exclaimed, her face reddening.

Kincaid rolled his eyes at her mischievously. "It feels like yesterday, now look at us. Soon we'll be picking out names!"

"Speaking of... I had an idea for one today in the shower," Emily quipped.

"Oh, yeah? Do tell, my love," Kincaid inquired.

"I was thinking Rose... after your grandmother," Emily replied.

"Rose... Rose Kincaid. I like it," he said.

"You do!" Emily squealed, looking up at him, her eyes filled with joy.

He nodded.

Emily smiled and leaned back into him, neatly fitting in the crook of his arm. Her body relaxed, perfectly and utterly content. It always amazed him. He placed his hands around her stomach, holding his family and feeling so in love.

The sound of a breaking news bulletin from the TV interrupted the moment.

A female Asian reporter in a trim charcoal-gray suit appeared, her eyeliner already running with tears. Ming Nguyen, the head anchor for CNN.

"Hello, all, we have some sad breaking news for you. We've just learned Hiroshi Takahashi, creator of SCAPE and founder and chairman of its namesake company, has passed away. He was eighty-four. We go to our tech correspondent Melissa Burgess for more. Melissa."

Kincaid's heart sank. Emily grasped his arm tightly, turning to him, tears already falling.

It can't be. We hadn't even told him the news—

Kincaid's eyes moved toward a large photo hanging in their hallway. It was of their wedding. Emily resplendent in a glittering white dress, he looking trim and fit in a tuxedo, and between them, in a traditional kimono, grinning like a proud parent, was Hiroshi. His vision blurred. Tears formed.

"Hello, Ming. Sources say Hiroshi was vacationing at his villa in Thailand, one of his many homes around the world, when he suddenly took ill. He was rushed to an area hospital, but by then, it was too late. He passed earlier this morning. We have no official word yet on cause of death and will update you once we do. This is Melissa Burgess, CNN."

"Thank you, Melissa," Ming said. "Now we'd like to bring in our panel, Don Stuart and Candice Lopez. Don, Candice, your reactions?"

Don and Candice appeared on the screen, each in tears. "I'm stunned," Don said, wiping his eyes theatrically. "We've lost a legend, a titan of technology who utterly transformed the world."

Candice nodded. "I'm also in shock. this is a man responsible for one of the greatest technological advances since perhaps the internet itself. But I can't help but wonder..."

"Wonder what?" Ming said, now in a split screen with Candice and Don, each in a tight head shot.

"Well," Candice inhaled, "I find it a bit odd. This is a man who had more money than God, a known health freak who was rumored to be undergoing special gene therapy and whose own mother lived well into her nineties."

"I think it just shows money isn't everything," Don interrupted.

Candice held up her hand. "Perhaps, but still, the timing is suspicious. Despite his significant wealth and influence, the man had his enemies."

"Candice, surely you aren't suggesting Hiroshi Takahashi was... murdered?" Ming uttered, her eyes lighting up, imagining the ratings spike.

"I'm saying it's not out of the realm of possibility," Candice insisted. "It's too early to say anything, but until we know more, I think we should consider all possibilities."

Emily turned to Kincaid. "Honey, there's no way..." she breathed.

"I... don't know. You've seen the succession plan. It's a mess. What even is a multinational trust?" Kincaid replied.

"But couldn't you step in?" she asked. "The board surely..."

"The board barely knows I exist," Kincaid emphasized. "They think I'm just some kind of wunderkind who Hiroshi was obsessed with for far too long. If I try and make a move now, there's no telling how they'd react. My access, Apex's agreement, your job, all of it could be thrown away, and we can't risk anything right now. We have to be smart... for Rose."

Emily curled into him tighter, her jaw clenched with worry and underneath that... fear.

"Excuse me, Candice," Ming's voice rang out. "I'm told we have more breaking news."

The screen shifted to a side-by-side of Ming and a large black building in the woods, surrounded by a pluming pillar of smoke.

"I'm told we've just received reports of a massive explosion at a data center in West Virginia. And..." she said, holding her hand to her eyepiece, her face darkening, "It appears there's been several more explosions at data centers around the world. We've—"

The screen went fuzzy and was replaced by a black screen with a bright yellow logo, made of six hexagons.

A robotic voice said, "Citizens of the world, for too long your governments have looked down upon and taken advantage of you. As billions of us have shifted our lives toward and into SCAPE, there is no universal framework for your rights to be protected. HIVE was formed to help represent the voices of everyone in and out of SCAPE. We have created a framework of equality and progress for everyone and have brought this to the governments of the world in good faith. Yet, none have listened. So in the best interest of our members, HIVE has forcibly taken control of all of SCAPE's data centers around the world. We will hold these data centers hostage until the governments of the world recognize our sovereignty as an independent collective."

Kincaid and Emily stared at each other in shock.

Since its release, more and more of the world worked, learned, and explored in SCAPE. It was the backbone of society. But without its data centers cycling through terabytes of information, the bandwidth of the system would plummet. People would panic, economies would collapse, chaos would reign.

The city below began to stir, piercing car horns, sirens, yells, shouts, glass shattering, and gunfire. Emily and Kincaid looked at one another again, both now with fear in their eyes as the memory shifted and shattered.

~~

The memory swirled, settling to another larger apartment. An office came into view. Kincaid was curled around his office chair, analyzing a code matrix with a steaming cup of coffee in hand. He looked older than before, his face beginning to wear the lines of stress, late nights, and age well.

The world seemed calmer than it had last, the city tamer, yet still a sense of unrest clinging to the air.

A phone ring echoed from the ceiling, his voice assistant chiming.

Video Call from: H. Co.

"Ignore," Kincaid said, the chiming ceasing. He sipped his coffee, savoring the nutty bold flavors and the silence in the house. Emily and Rose were due back with groceries at any moment, and with it, the chaos only a preschooler can bring.

As Rose grew bigger, so too did her demands on his attention. Moments of silence where he could truly work were becoming rare. Not that he needed to work much anyway; his years of designing and coding for both Apex and SCAPE had left him and Emily comfortable. The only thing that kept him coming back was his obsession with creating order and beauty, trapped in lines of code.

The phone rang once more. H. Co echoing again from his assistant.

Ugh.

Frustrated, Kincaid swiped with his hand, accepting the video call. A screen popped up on the wall of his study. As the picture loaded, a young Hispanic man with brown eyes and just the hint of a goatee appeared in the frame.

"Yes?" Kincaid asked.

The young man cleared his throat. "Hello, is this Mr. Dashiell Kincaid?"

"Yes, this is he," Kincaid replied.

"You're a tough man to get a hold of Mr. Kincaid. My office has made multiple attempts to contact you with no success, so I figured I would reach out personally. My name is Luis Garza; I'm the head of Government Relations at HIVE. How are you today?"

"Good, what is this about?" Kincaid inquired.

"It's about the proposal my office has for you, sir," Garza replied.

"Sorry, I haven't seen any kind of proposal. I've been very busy, you see," Kincaid remarked.

"*Sí, Sí,* I understand completely. Some might construe the use of the word busy on calls such as this as lack of interest or even worse, outright rudeness. But I always say, you never know what's going on in a person's life until you sit down and chat *cara a cara.* All of those wonderful projects you're working on, not to mention being a dedicated family man. You have a daughter, no?" Garza asked.

"Yes, Rose." Kincaid smiled. "She just turned five." His eyes flicked to a photo on his desk. It was of Emily, Rose, and him on her fourth birthday. That day, they went down to Central Park to feed the ducks and afterward posed on Gapstow Bridge. Rose was on his shoulders, her face thrown back in a grin. Her pale blue eyes twinkling the light, she held a bright pink balloon in one hand, which matched her pink jacket. Emily wore a red cardigan sweater and jeans. She was also smiling, her arms deeply interlocked into his own.

"*Magnífico.* Congratulations. They do grow so fast," Garza said.

"So what is this proposal, Mr. Garza?" Kincaid sighed.

"Well, it's quite simple, really. We'd like you to come work for HIVE. You'd be our SCAPE consultant. As you may have heard, we are on the verge of our billionth member. As the representatives for the SCAPE-user rights worldwide, we highly value the knowledge and expertise someone of your stature would bring to our organization," Garza declared.

"I'm sorry, Mr. Garza. I'm afraid I'm quite happy where I am. Now, if you'll excuse—"

"Please, hear me out, sir. I think you'll find if you give me just five more minutes of your time, you'll be more intrigued," Garza pleaded.

"I'm sorry, Mr. Garza, as wonderful as that all sounds, to be completely honest with you, I can't bring myself to work for a terrorist collective masquerading as a political party."

Garza's eyes shone, as if he were about to burst into tears. "Chairman Lintz has made it clear: we are *not* terrorists. We are simply the next step in governance. As the world becomes more interconnected and immersed in the wonders of SCAPE, people's rights need protection. If we don't band together now, the governments of the world can and will take advantage of us. That is why HIVE had to take control of those data centers, to force the governments of the world to come to the table and listen. Together, we can all prosper and thrive."

"Mr. Garza. Put whatever spin on it you want but my answer has not changed. Good day," Kincaid said, swiping his hand in front of the screen to end the call. But instead of the screen vanishing, it remained active. He waved his hand several more times with no effect.

Garza watched the whole scene, sighed deeply, and closed his eyes. When he opened them again his entire face had changed, all the warmth vanishing. "Well, that's very unfortunate. Very unfortunate indeed."

A tiny screen appeared below his face. It was drone footage of the highway, the shot centered on a white car. The image dipped down and its license plate came into view. A chill ran through Kincaid. The license plate was his own, his wife and daughter inside.

"What the fuck is this?" Kincaid uttered, his heart beginning to pound.

"Just watch," Garza purred.

The image zoomed out and two black cars came into frame, gaining on his. One pulled into the other lane, sped by, and cut in front of his wife. She managed to slam on the breaks, stopping just inches from the rear bumper. The other pulled up behind. The doors opened and men in black suits filed out. They knocked on the window of the car.

Don't open the door, Em.

They stood there a moment, before one man reached into his jacket, pulled out a dark object, and slammed it into the window, shattering it. He reached in and unlocked the door, then pulled Emily out. She was kicking and screaming. One man smacked her in the head, causing her to go limp, while another reached in the back and grabbed Rose, car seat and all. Kincaid could see the confusion on her face.

"Emily! Rose!" he shouted, jumping up from his seat, his face inches from the screen.

The men retreated into the vehicles, the doors slamming, and the image went black. Only Garza remained, his face impassive.

"What the fuck do you want?" Kincaid demanded, his voice breaking with rage.

"I'll make this very simple: come and work for us, or watch your family die," Garza replied.

"You wouldn't *dare*," Kincaid seethed.

Garza's eyebrow raised. "Dare? Oh, trust me, Mr. Kincaid. We are willing to go to lengths you can only dream of to accomplish our goals." Garza's eyes were flat and business-like.

"And I fit into those, how?" Kincaid queried.

Garza smiled, a sly sinister grin like a fox finding an unlocked henhouse.

"You are *essential*. You, Dashiell Kincaid, darling and protegee of none other than Hiroshi Takahashi himself. A man who, by many accounts in both the virtual and real world, is the only person left alive who knows SCAPE as well as its creator, perhaps even more so. Not only that, but someone who still has access to SCAPE's root systems and with the right amount of motivation, can make changes that will affect everything," Garza exclaimed.

"I can't just change the root system overnight. It will take weeks, months. Not to mention the safeguards. It's impossible," Kincaid cried.

"As much as I want to believe your feeble attempts at excuses, we simply do not have the time," Garza said, as the doorbell rang. "Ah, I believe that's your motivation, now."

Kincaid walked toward the door and opened it; a small, unmarked package lay on the stoop.

He walked back to the screen. "Go on, open it," Garza whispered, leaning closer to the camera.

Kincaid began tearing into the packaging, while Garza explained, "In the *barrios* where I grew up, the cartels had a special way of sending a message. When I was younger, I found it barbaric, but as I've aged, I've come to appreciate the subtlety..."

Kincaid tore off the last of the packaging, revealing a small white ring box. He opened it and almost dropped it to the floor in shock. Inside was Emily's finger, her wedding ring still attached. Curled around it was a tiny locket of brown hair, and nestled in between was Rose's favorite pink bow.

Kincaid stumbled over to his desk, catching his ashen face in the reflection of the glass tabletop as his knees failed him and wobbled.

"I believe I have your full attention now, no?" Garza mused.

Kincaid nodded, his knuckles white.

"Good, here's what you need to do. You will change the admin access of the banking, health, agriculture, and defense access points within SCAPE. You need to make it look like HIVE hacked in and took some major piece of data. When the government finds this, they will attempt to fix it but when they do, you will implant a virus that will not only lock them out of access in to their systems in SCAPE but will attempt to take control of their other systems. They naturally will rush to defend themselves, and in their haste will not realize we've already won the true prize."

"You'll never get away with this. SCAPE can't be taken control of so easily. You have no idea the fail safes that exist," Kincaid uttered.

"Oh, but *you do*, don't you, Mr. Kincaid? That's why you are working for us. You'll continue to monitor SCAPE, resolving problems and issues like before but instead, for us, our agenda. We'll be three steps ahead of them the entire time. Besides, you seem to misunderstand; the prize isn't SCAPE itself or even the people who use it. It's the world they're leaving behind. You have three weeks; any significant delays and you'll find more of those packages on your doorstep, though I can't quite say what will be in them. It'll be your special little surprise. Good day, Mr. Kincaid," Garza growled before smiling and ending the call.

The memory shifted into code. There was a giant shake and the world went white, along with a feeling of being pulled upward through a long twisting straw.

~~~

PART 3

CHAPTER 15

———

Screeching tires and whining brakes awoke Kincaid.

At first, the world was flat, all blurry shapes and rough outlines before settling into the ceiling of a white van.

The heat of the battery engine radiated through the floor onto his skin. Sweat trickled off his brow.

Wait. I can feel heat. Am I...?

Kincaid jolted up, hitting his head on the rear door handle. The pain was instant, blinding, and bloody. He was back in the real world.

He wiped the blood from his brow, his limbs still tingling like waking up from hours of being asleep. Small black and blue bruises dotted his arms, legs, and torso, signs of an extended and strenuous session in the rig. His head ached with pain and the burden of forgotten memories, now found.

"Sugar, you look rougher than road kill left out in the summer heat," a voice remarked.

Dawn sat across from him wearing a bulletproof vest, a large shotgun resting across her legs. Large boxes surrounded them on either side.

More pain radiated through his head, followed by a flash of memory. Emily and his wedding. He remembered hugging someone in the bridal party; she had blond hair and amber eyes. She and Dawn shared the smile, eyes, cheekbones, and laugh.

"Dawn? Wait, you're... my sister-in-law?" Kincaid choked out.

"Bet you feel bad about not giving me overtime now!" Dawn grinned, looking like Emily for a moment. He couldn't believe it.

"But how? Why? What's going on?" Kincaid gasped.

Dawn tossed him a tiny bottle of whiskey. He barely managed to catch it, his coordination still groggy.

"Drink that. After a few sips, we'll catch up *for real*," Dawn commanded.

Kincaid unscrewed the cap and drank half the bottle. It burned like cheap ass whiskey, but the shock sharpened his focus a bit. He coughed, rubbing some that had dripped out the corner of his mouth.

"How the hell did you find me?" he asked.

"Well," Dawn said, reaching under her vest into her bra and pulling something out. She motioned for him to hold out his hand and into it, she gently placed his AI implant. The circuits within were still and gray. His eyes watered.

"Snoops," Kincaid whispered; his hand closed around the implant and squeezed.

"It took two days, but eventually, Snoops managed to send out an encrypted distress call to the receiver in the office, right before its signal went offline. Took us a minute to triangulate you in Old Downtown. This strange smoke kept interfering with our sensors. We busted in there, almost got killed by that crazy Asian Distro doctor. Thought we were some sort of fuzz. Took some persuading but eventually, he led us to you. You were wrapped up in that rig tighter than a swaddled newborn, and your implants were literally smoking. The doctor freaked out and immediately pulled them out of you, said if they had been in there in any longer, you'd have brain damage. I took the opportunity to procure this lovely van from the good doctor's storage and pulled you up."

"I can't believe it... managed to do all that..." Kincaid muttered before trailing into silence.

Dawn nodded. "I did some scanning before you woke up. I'm not seeing any signs of activity at all. It's like the entire memory has been wiped."

A tear fell from his eye onto the implant, making the circuits within sparkle. He inhaled deeply. "That's because Snoops is gone; it/he/she sacrificed itself for me. Ended up in a Schrodinger loop because of it."

"I'm sorry, sugar. I know how much that AI meant to you. But it ultimately did its job as a military grade, which is to prioritize the safety of its host."

They sat there, letting the moment breathe.

Eventually, Kincaid snapped out of his daze. "Okay, I'm ready. Tell me what's going on?"

"Let's start with DK Consulting. How long have I been working there with you?" she asked.

Kincaid sat there for a moment, thinking back. "You've been with me at DK Consulting since the beginning. We took our first case ten years ago," Kincaid answered, his head pulsing as he did so, the signs of a headache forming.

Dawn shook her head. "I may look good for my age, but even I don't age *that* well. I've only been working with you for five years."

"What! Five years? But that doesn't make sense. I remember you being at the opening of DK right there cutting the ribbon with me, then on your first full day, demanding I buy you that damn antique microwave 'cause the new ones don't radiate food like they used to!" Kincaid exclaimed.

Dawn sighed. Her eyes clouded. "As much as I might agree with that microwave sentiment, I never said that, nor was I there at the opening. When I showed up, you had already won a few awards. The work was picking up, and you needed some help to manage it all."

"I—" Kincaid began, pain blooming between his eyes.

Dawn looked at him, concerned.

He continued, "How could I remember you being there, if you weren't?"

"Alex thinks HIVE somehow planted false memories into you. I don't really know the specifics, so you'll have to ask him that yourself," Dawn stated.

"Alex? You talked to him? We're going to see him, where?" Kincaid gasped.

"I talked to him yesterday. He said once you got out of SCAPE, you would have some of your old memories back and HIVE would be after you. So I'm taking you to an ANY-NONE safe house. Alex's been hiding out there ever since he faked his death."

"*Wait,* you knew he was alive, that the entire case was a lie?"

Dawn looked to the side, clenching her arm. "Not... at first. The Huntington murder truly was a shock to me, but when Maureen strolled in, I knew something was up."

"Maureen?"

"Alex's wife, they met a few years ago after your... disappearance."

"Disappearance?"

"Yes, shortly after HIVE took over the SCAPE data centers you... disappeared."

"Disappeared... why? Where would I have gone?" he asked.

"I wish I knew. You should probably wait to ask Alex; he might know or at least have a better idea than me," Dawn whispered, looking at her watch. "We'll be there soon."

"Will Emily and Rose be there?"

Dawn looked down again, her hair covering her face. Her body shook with sobs and when she looked up at him, her eyes were full of tears, causing her makeup to run.

No, Kincaid pleaded. *It can't be.*

Yet, as Kincaid sat there, he remembered the pain he felt in the labyrinth. The images in the pond, the girl in the fog. He realized his memory was trying to tell him something he had forgotten all along. That this pain that followed him had a familiar name: grief. Once he accepted that, the bottom dropped out, he bent over, tears pouring from his eyes. He let out a deep and guttural sob. When the waves subsided, another emotion lay waiting underneath: white-hot rage.

"When? How? *Garza!*" Kincaid shouted, his eyes wide and wild with fury. He scrambled toward the door, trying to rip the handle off with his teeth. Somehow, Dawn grabbed his shoulder and pulled him back down across the cab into her arms. He scratched against her sleeves, vest, and hair. With every flail, she held tighter, gently shushing him, until the anger shimmered down to a more manageable temp. He gently removed himself from her chest.

Dawn placed her hand on his shoulder and squeezed hard. "I know. I feel it too, every single damn day."

How long they could have stayed that way, they never knew. A bullet tore through the back door, passing just inches by their heads, ruining the moment.

"HIVE!" Dawn hissed. She slid back and banged three times on the cabin wall of the truck. Immediately, they picked up speed. She reached into her vest and threw out a tiny metallic sphere; it bounced once before magnetically attaching to the floor. She pressed her finger to her temple, and the sphere split into two, the halves flying a few feet apart. A tiny blue beam shot between them, then blurred and a holographic screen expanded.

The screen was blank for a second before settling into a tactical split-screen. The left side showed the rear camera view and the right a crude proximity radar with their route highlighted. Both pictures were grim.

The left showed three black armored SUVs gaining on them, a muscular man with a large rifle jammed out of the sun roof. The right showing their van as a moving yellow dot along a green route with ten red dots approaching from the north.

Dawn stared at the screen, panic filling her face. Her eyes flicked toward Kincaid, and the panic slowly gave way to steely determination. She smirked at him and cocked her shotgun.

"Pull some of those boxes down and use this," Dawn commanded, throwing him a set of bungee cords. "Tie them down right in front of the door for cover, then put another set down toward the back. When I tell you to, get the fuck behind that last row and don't come out until I say."

"I want to fight too," Kincaid pleaded.

She looked at him, her eyes full of an unknowable emotion. "You have some hero complex?" she barked. "Don't be a fucking martyr, sugar. Getting you to Alex *alive* is all that matters right now. Let me help get you there."

Kincaid nodded and began pulling boxes down. They were way heavier than he expected. He had just finished tying down the first row when another bullet tore through the door, missing his head by inches and disappearing into the floor of the van. A metallic odor wafted from the hole.

"Get down! Idiot," Dawn hissed, her eyes returning to the screen. Two other SUVs appeared behind, sped up, and flanked around the first. Their sunroofs opened. Two large men emerged with shiny metallic guns, guns Kincaid recognized.

"Tell the driver to serpentine, now!" Kincaid bellowed.

Dawn banged twice on the wall, and the van swerved right just as they pulled the trigger.

Two blue flashes obliterated the road where the van just was. Chunks of asphalt rained on the roof like deadly hail. The screen flickered in and out.

"What the hell was that?" Dawn yelled.

"Thumpers!" Kincaid warned.

"*Fuck*, are you serious? Those assholes aren't playing. Get behind me now!"

Kincaid scrambled behind her over another row of boxes. Dawn slid by him over to the back doors. Using the barrel of her shotgun, she knocked the latch, flinging the doors open. Sunlight flooded in, blinding them both. She managed to duck down as bullets rained in, peppering the van like poppy seeds on a bagel. Dawn waited for the volley to die down, then popped up and pulled the trigger.

The shotgun belched a round straight into the windshield of the lead SUV, shattering the glass instantly. It shook as the other fanned outward to avoid the glass.

Dawn unloaded another round, hitting one of the men in the shoulder, the impact causing him to lose grip of his Thumper. The other SUV moved in. Sensing an opportunity, Dawn aimed and fired toward the left tire. It burst like confetti, the rim hitting the pavement with a shower of sparks. The SUV wobbled then careened to the left, broadsiding the other SUV into a wall. The one behind them swerved, hit more debris, and ended up meeting the business end of a street light. The other man with the Thumper flew from the sunroof, while the driver tumbled through the windshield. Both hit the pavement with a sickening crunch.

"Nice shooting!" Kincaid cheered.

Dawn grinned as they watched the crash grow smaller. She glanced back at the radar. Three of the red dots had stopped. The others seemed missing for a moment before they reappeared, now closing in from ahead of them.

The van shuddered and lost speed. The metallic odor was stronger now. Dawn sniffed, then pressed her finger down on her temple.

"Denny, what's the deal?" she demanded. She listened for a response. "They hit what?" Dawn cursed, glancing back at the radar. "Fuck it, we're going to plan B."

Kincaid flew into the wall as the van swerved to the left, barely scraping its way into a narrow alley.

Dawn bent down and tapped on one half of the sphere. The screen faded, and the halves snapped back together. She held it out to him.

Kincaid's fingers had just touched it when she said, "Sugar, listen to me. At the end of this alley, there's a hover-bike. You'll take that bike into the old subway. Your route to Alex is in this data sphere."

"But what about you?" Kincaid asked.

She shook her head. "There's too many of them. They'll be on us before we know it. We'll buy you time; you *have* to get to Alex. Once there, you'll be safe."

"You'll never take that many guys out. Especially if they have Thumpers. I can't lose you, not when I've just found you again," he whispered.

"Kincaid," Dawn explained, pressing the sphere into his hand. "Remember *I* signed up for this, for myself, for Em and Rose, for revenge. If today is the day I go, I'll at least take some of these HIVE mother fuckers with me. Besides, if I survive, just *think* of the workers comp you'll give me!"

Kincaid smiled right before the world went vertical. Dawn, the van, and him floated midair, suspended in confusion before slamming back to earth. Twisted metal, burnt wires, and gravity greeted them before the darkness.

Kincaid awoke, pulling his head from the wall of the car. A patch of blood marked his presence. Boxes pressed into his flesh. He shakily shoved them aside and got his bearings. The van was on its side. The metallic odor was now sharper, fluid trickled somewhere, and steam hissed. Somehow, he was still clutching the sphere.

"Dawn?" Kincaid muttered, looking around the cabin. No response. He crawled over the edge of the door and fell onto the street. His side screamed with pain, every breath hurting like hot lances to his lungs. He tried getting up, but his right leg crumbled, throbbing. His vision blurred.

More boxes were flung into the street, their contents strewn everywhere. Kincaid huffed and shoved through the debris with his one good leg, shouting for Dawn, ignoring the pain as he did so.

"Sugar," Dawn weakly replied.

Kincaid limped toward the noise.

Dawn was hunched up against the wall. One leg was twisted and broken, her right shoulder crushed and spewing pools of blood. A deep gash ran through her face, bright bruises already forming. Her breathing was shallow and labored.

Kincaid bent down and gently placed a hand on her neck. Her pulse fluttered, erratic and in shock.

She looked at him and heaved, "You... need to get to... bike." She coughed, blood dribbling out of her mouth. She inclined her head toward the left. He followed her nod, and there on the corner, miraculously unscathed, was the hover bike.

Tire squeals drew their attention.

Two SUVs were flying, single-file, down the alley. Dawn gasped and peeled herself from the wall and with her one good arm, scraping her nails against the pavement, pulled herself toward the shotgun that lay a few feet beyond, leaving a trail of blood behind her. She reached it, heaving, and coughed more blood. Somehow, she flipped it up onto a fallen box in front of her and aimed it toward the oncoming vehicles. She bent down and used her chin to cock it.

"Go... make them pay," Dawn demanded.

Kincaid nodded, tears falling from his eyes as he limped toward the hover bike. Grimacing, he flung his leg over the seat. He pressed the start button, the engine humming to life as the bike lifted off the ground. He placed the sphere into the center console, and the map loaded over the display. The path took him down into an abandoned subway station. The entrance to the station was just beyond the bike.

Two blue flashes flew overhead, shattering the wall above him. Kincaid gunned the throttle, and the bike flew toward the entrance. A single shotgun shot rang out as he entered into the underground.

~~~

CHAPTER 16

Kincaid flew through the tunnel, lights flashing by in random intervals. The glow of the map illuminated his face like a halo. The route grew shorter and shorter. Eventually, he came to the end, and it opened up into an underground mall. Faded and rusting coffee, barber, tailor, and food court signs hung loosely on the walls, the glass store fronts shattered or completely gone, and the once-proud gleaming white subway tile that decorated the space was now snaked with cracks and mold. Any remaining exposed metal had long since been claimed by oxidation. Old piles of plastic trash littered the floor. Water dripped from a broken pipe above to his left. Large rats, feral cats, and dogs congregated around it like it was a watering hole in the Serengeti. They eyed him boldly, as if daring him to come and take it from them.

The bike continued through the square, stopping at a corroded escalator, half of its steps either missing or gone. The gears within were exposed like a skeleton. At the top stood two large muscular men holding assault rifles. Spotting Kincaid, they pressed their fingers to their temples, radioing in his arrival.

They threw down a rope ladder from the edge and motioned for Kincaid to climb. He grasped the rungs and pulled himself up. Scrambling over the ledge, he realized they stood in front of an old gym, its purple neon sign lacking letters. They gestured for him to walk inside, following as he did. Kincaid entered, marveling at how the scent of copper and old sweat still clung to the room, as if sealed there by the collective effort of its past patrons. They moved past crumpled ellipticals, treadmills, kettle-bells, and weight machines into the old yoga studio, its mirrors cracked. Lights flickered on overhead, revealing a running track that circled above an old manager's office and entrances to the locker rooms. In the center of the floor sat a small wooden table and two chairs.

One of the men left Kincaid's side and climbed up the stairs that shrieked with his weight and went into the office beyond. A light turned on within. The other stood behind him, breathing heavily. A few minutes went by when the man held his hand up to his head, muttered something, and walked away, leaving Kincaid to stare at himself in the broken, grimy mirrors, alone.

"After all these years... Finally, we meet face to face in the real," a deep voice said.

Kincaid raised his head to the balcony above as Alex emerged from the doorway. The young man Kincaid last saw in the memory had aged.

Alex's blond hair had dimmed, now streaked with strands of brown and gray. His face was no longer a healthy tan but pale and lined. Large dark circles rested under his eyes. He was gaunt, shoulder bones visible through his loose-fitted blazer. A crumbled, wrinkled dress shirt lay half open beneath, revealing blue circular bruises. He walked gingerly down the stairs, as if his limbs weren't his own. He held out his hand, and Kincaid shook it and was shocked at the cool leathery texture of his skin. Alex gestured to the small wooden table in the corner, the two chairs poised.

They sat, Alex with a visible grimace. He reached into his blazer pocket and pulled out a pack of joints. He carefully opened the carton, offered one to Kincaid, who shook his head. Alex shrugged and put one between his teeth and pulled. The joint's tip lit automatically. He coughed and exhaled a sweet smoke that plumed around them.

"Sorry," Alex rasped. "It helps with the pain..."

"What happened to you?" Kincaid asked.

Alex pulled again, exhaling with a sigh. "It's been a long journey. I've spent weeks and months at a time in SCAPE. Searching, guiding, planning. Despite the marvels of modern technology, all of that eventually took its toll. Normally, I would convalesce somewhere fancy with Maureen but given the current scenario," Alex commented, gesturing to the entire room, "I've been unable to do so."

"Oh, how the mighty have fallen," Kincaid quipped.

Alex sat back and cocked his head to the side. "Amazing..." he said, reaching across the table, cupping Kincaid's cheek and brushing his hair. "You sound just like him." He stared deeply into Kincaid's eyes, while his own only held sadness and pain.

The display of affection stunned Kincaid. He recoiled, scraping the chair against the concrete floor.

"I'm sorry. I didn't mean to startle you; it's just so strange," Alex whispered.

"Strange?" Kincaid queried.

"You and I are only six months apart in age, yet, here I am looking like shit but you... You look as good as the last time I saw you over fifteen years ago," Alex asserted.

"Fifteen years? Are you sure?" Kincaid gasped.

"Quite. We had just celebrated Rose's fifth birthday. You were egging me on to settle down so you didn't have to parent alone," Alex commented, chuckling at the memory.

"But that doesn't—"

Alex held up his hand. He took a deep drag on the joint, its cherry glow lighting his face in orange shadows, making him look like a ghoul. He exhaled and continued, "I've been holding something back from you, the final piece in the puzzle. It's the reason why you have scattered memories of the past, your accident, why you didn't remember what happened to Rose and Emily. Why you didn't remember me at all."

"What?" Kincaid asked

"It's best you hear it from yourself," Alex said and held up an old iPhone and placed it on the table. He turned it on and navigated to the voicemail section. He spun the phone toward Kincaid and motioned to the first item in the list. The entry read *D. Kincaid 03/12/2035*; it was thirty seconds long. Alex motioned for him to press play.

Kincaid heard muffled sounds at first, then his voice:

"Alex, it's me. I don't have much time. Rose and Em are... dead. HIVE... killed them. They blackmailed me into working for them, switching all of SCAPE's admin access over to them. They're going to use it to force the government to bow to their demands. I'm going to try and stop them, but if I fail, there's something I need you to do, something I need you to find. Hiroshi and I built a failsafe that can stop all of this for good. We hid our memories of its creation and ultimate location in SCAPE in case we were ever compromised and to ensure it stayed safe. There are mazes, tunnels, clues. The first clue is layered over my old Mortal Kombat X disk. You need to execute a move combo to unlock the first data file. Good luck and if, for some reason, I don't make it back, know I love you man—"

The message cut off, ending in static.

Kincaid straightened to Alex's face running with tears. Alex sniffled, the joint burning his fingertips, yet he seemed to not notice.

"That... was the last time I spoke to my friend," Alex uttered, wiping his eyes.

What? I'm right here.

The longer he sat there, a feeling began to unfurl. As it blew through the windmills of his mind, he perceived its shape, its feeling, and realized he had felt it ever since he saw Wendell's body, all those days ago.

Alex read his face, took another long drag on his now diminished joint, and said the words that echoed in Kincaid's heart, "Dashiell Kincaid was killed shortly after this message."

"Bullshit," Kincaid retorted.

Alex smirked. "I suppose if I was faced with an existential mirror, I'd reply the same way. But you are here, aren't you?"

"I'm here because of you!" Kincaid shouted.

Alex took another drag and replied, "Yes, you are. But that doesn't mean you don't have doubts, or did they not program those in?"

Kincaid leaned back in his chair. He wanted to not believe it, to spit in Alex's face, to bemoan the whole thing as a lie, a trick, a shadow. But he couldn't. His memories *were* patchy. Some just blank, empty things. He realized outside of the memories he gained in SCAPE, he couldn't think back more than ten years ago and if Dawn was right, how many of *those* years were actually real? His head began to pound, signaling its simultaneous treachery and defeat. The only voice left in his mind yelled but one thing: *impostor.*

"So then I'm a...?" he asked, hoping what he'd heard before was a fantasy.

"You're a pale echo of who he was, made by the very people who killed him. A clone puppet made solely to lead HIVE to me and the Terminal Code," Alex coldly stated.

Kincaid gasped and held his head in his hands. His inner voice's comment in SCAPE echoed: *Quite the Pinocchio, aren't you?* He couldn't believe it. "How am I sitting here then? What am I?" he mumbled into his palms.

"You'll have to ask HIVE," Alex replied, reaching over to pull Kincaid's hands apart. "Lucky for you, that's exactly where you're going. Straight into the bees' nest to spray the Terminal Code."

Kincaid lifted his head. "What did you say?"

Alex sighed then cleared his throat. "Look, I have no idea how you're feeling right now. But there's no more time for questions. We need to act, *now*. In case you haven't noticed, HIVE hasn't just taken over the entire city, they've taken over the entire world. HIVE runs every city managing, manipulating, slowly taking pieces of real infrastructure, real power, real control. Bit by bit, they amass and consume until you, like a dog, are suddenly outside, begging for scraps. SCAPE may have been how they were born, but now they are using it to exploit and steal from those who still have things left and use you to help hide their crimes! If everyone is enthralled with a virtual world, who controls the real one? This code is the only thing that will stop them."

"But the code will destroy SCAPE forever! Not to mention kill millions, billions of people..." Kincaid sputtered.

"Not everyone will die, only a portion. The rest will wake up to my report on what HIVE really is. What they've done to this world and to the people left behind in it."

"But the cost is too high. There has to be some other way," Kincaid pleaded.

"There is *no* other way!" Alex shouted, leaping to his feet. He bent down closer to Kincaid, his eyes blazing with fury. "I've spent *years* looking for this code. Waiting. To avenge my friend. To stop the organization that killed his family, killed him, cloned him, twisted his obsession with order, fed by his childhood traumas, into helping them slowly eat the world from within the system he helped to refine. No, they need to be stopped; they need to be revealed for what they are. I'd rather suffer the death of billions than domination by the few."

Kincaid recalled the feeling of those few memories of Alex he did have: the joy and laughter of the young boy, the ambition of the young man. When he looked at the man before him and what he had become, he felt only pity, and rage.

"Why do you need me, then? Don't you have the code already? Why not just do it yourself?" Kincaid mocked with disgust.

"Trust me, if I could, I would've a long time ago. But as you heard, the original Kincaid hid the code in pieces. Each part of the puzzle contained a different piece, a different function, all guarded by different AIs he programmed himself. Before he was murdered, HIVE interrogated him and found out about the code somehow, specifically the last piece. They freaked out, and dug deeper into his mind, trying to find the answers. But by the time they figured out the encryption he placed on it was so advanced only *he* could break it, he had already died. They attempted reasoning with the AI but they could never meet its conditions. The only way they could access it was through a clone of him. When you slayed the Minotaur and unlocked the memories, the last piece of the code was embedded into your Avatar's root matrix."

"How do you know all of this?" Kincaid asked.

Alex was silent for a moment, his eyes lost in memory. "Because... I tried to save him. I broke into where they were holding him with some friends, the precursor to ANY-NONE, but by the time we got there, we were too late. After, I tore the place apart, tortured people, eventually found the surveillance video."

"I don't care if you need me. I won't do it," Kincaid uttered.

"Not even for Rose and Emily, for revenge against Garza?" Alex asked, his voice wavering.

Kincaid thought of Rose and Emily. The grief he had felt earlier. The joy. Then came the questions. Were those memories really even his? Were those feelings? His head flared, and he gripped the table. He didn't know; he could never know. The only thing he kept coming back to was, were the lives of billions worth revenge over phantom's memories?

"No," he replied.

Alex roared and launched himself across the table, grabbing Kincaid by his shirt and pulling his face inches from his own. The guards running out from above pointed guns down at both of them.

"Whatever your memories are, whatever your beliefs, I know you've seen this city," Alex hissed, his face turning red and his spit flying in Kincaid's face. "I know you've seen the rot, the poverty, the fear. HIVE is *not* for the people. You know this. You've felt this. What's worse: they are using something you love to hurt people. Despite being a clone, that's something you share with my friend. Your love of SCAPE is undeniable. Will you really let HIVE distort the beauty and order of a beautiful system, of hundreds of virtual worlds and this one to their own ends? Are you going to let them get away with *that*?"

An anger welled up from within Kincaid. He thought of SCAPE, of PRMARAVE, Clue Town, and Murder Alley,

FANTASCAPE, and many of the hundreds of other worlds and zones. He thought of the people, the things they could do, the things they could be. The freedom, the joy, the potential. A universe of such infinite possibilities distorted. Something within him raged at the thought. Though his doubts remained, his mind swirled with lingering questions. As he pondered, one thing became clear: he had to find more answers and the only way to do that was to play along.

"No, I can't," Kincaid said quietly.

Alex exhaled deeply and let go of his shirt, shrinking back down into an even frailer version of himself, his anger draining him completely.

"Good, good. Here's what you need to do. For the code to work, it needs to be installed into the base layer of the system update. When it goes live, it will spread throughout all of SCAPE. Problem is HIVE has forced SCAPE to do all system updates under their supervision. You'll need to sneak into the government building and log into SCAPE from there. Then you'll upload the code into the update. Then send me a ping."

"What about you? Your part of the code?" Kincaid asked.

"ANYNONE and I will create a distraction in the Cluster. It will draw HIVE's attention away from you, long enough for you to enter it in. Once they take the bait, and I get your ping, I'll log in myself. The ping will bring me right to you. Once together in SCAPE, our pieces of code should resonate and self-assemble and boom, mission complete," Alex stated.

"How do I get in?" Kincaid asked.

Alex smirked. "You think we picked this place at random? There's an access tunnel that leads from here straight into the sewer system beneath the Cluster. There's an access point we've already secured that goes right into the HIVE building. Then once inside, use this," he said, handing Kincaid a small red access badge. "Got this from a friend, should get you to the upload area. Once there, we'll upload it right under their noses."

Kincaid nodded.

"Excellent," Alex chirped, slapping his hand against Kincaid's shoulder.

"Get ready, you leave in ten. The update goes live in a few hours."

~~~

CHAPTER 17

Kincaid slinked through the tunnels, his only company cat-sized rats.

They shrieked as he approached, running from the beam of his head-lamp that cut through the darkness. He constantly had to look down, his footing just a narrow strip of concrete. One misstep and he'd fall into the steady stream of sewer water that flowed to his left. The worst thing was the smell. It penetrated everything, his nose, eyes, clothes, socks, and shoes. He worried it would alert HIVE to his presence.

The tunnel slowly sloped upward, allowing gravity to help carry the water to the processing plant deep beyond. As he neared the Cluster, the slope became more pronounced. He slipped. Scrambling, he ran his hands against the wall, looking for something to hold onto. Luckily, he found rusted handrails and pulled against them, the cold and slimy metal digging into the palms of his hands.

Great. I'll probably get an infection. Then as he pondered on it more, he realized he actually didn't know if he would get an infection. Did clones or whatever he was get infections?

Kincaid shrugged and continued pulling himself along the tunnel.

The ceiling overhead narrowed toward him, the light of his head lamp hitting it more and more. Eventually, it caught the edge of something reflective, nearly blinding him. Hesitantly, he ran his light over it again and realized it was a marker for a brass sign on the ceiling that read:

Central Square .5 mi

Close.
Kincaid came to a metal ladder that went up and over a concrete ledge. A faint orange light filtered over the top. He flashed his head beam on the ceiling. Another brass sign read:

Central Square ↑

He grabbed the first rung and climbed. He pulled himself onto a concrete platform that led to a large, heavy fire door. He approached the door; wires hung from the alarm box above it, their edges hastily cut. An old wooden wedge was lodged in-between the door and the jamb.

He shoved the heavy door aside and saw a large metal staircase winding upward. Red utility lights gleamed, painting the white concrete bricks pink.

Kincaid walked up them and emerged into a wooden structure covered in a blue tarp, a construction entrance into the HIVE building. A breeze sneaked through one of the edges, a pale beam of sunlight shot in. He peeked through; the center of the Cluster lay just beyond. The Portal glimmered in the sunlight across the square, its form today a large white-stone tower, a holographic Lighthouse of Alexandria. Its mirror shone like a star near the apex, obscuring the golden statue perched above it and lit the entire square below with shifting reflections. A bright holographic sign hovered out in front of it, reading:

Time to Update: 30 min

He hurried through the construction entrance into the HIVE building. The inside was cold, his breath visible. The interior was a Brutalist design, large pillars of concrete, dark glass, exposed pipes. Lights were embedded in the floor at evenly spaced intervals, lighting the wall in patches. It gave the entire room a long and eerie feeling. A yellow runner rug stitched with the HIVE logo lay in the middle of the dark concrete floor. He followed it down the hallway.

Halfway through, a loud bang shook the room, the glass vibrating. Doors whooshed open ahead. Kincaid hid behind a column as large, hulking security bots flew out, their faces red. They were followed by several android and human security guards. He began to move from the column when the slow, methodical clap of shoes on the floor stopped him.

Kincaid strained to hear its location. He couldn't tell where it was coming from; the only thing he knew for certain was it was getting closer.

Clap.

He frantically looked around and ran toward the nearest door, swiping his access badge over the reader. The panel flashed red.

Clap.

Panicking, he ran toward the second nearest door and waved the badge. Luckily, the panel turned green but the door only slid open an inch. Flabbergasted, he threw his hands over the edge and pulled; the door slowly moved as if its track were frozen solid.

Clap.

The door was a quarter of the way open. Murmurs of voices reached his ears.

Kincaid spun sideways and jammed his body through the doorway, his face scraping against the frame. He waved the badge over the access panel on the other side and the door slowly began to close. The voices now were louder, as if they were right in front of him. Curious, he peeked around the edge.

A coterie walked through the hall, all wearing dark suits and chatting animatedly. Their attention focused on something or someone in the center. The crowd parted for a moment and in the middle stood Mayor Garza. His gold eyes wandered from aide to aide as he barked out instructions. They hung on his every word, nodding fiercely. A single strand of his hair had fallen from its coiffed position. His eyes flicked toward the closing door and narrowed. Kincaid pulled his eye back.

Kincaid waited and listened. The crowd still chatted loudly just outside. He carefully peeked around the edge again. Garza was staring directly at the door. As the crowd around him remained oblivious, he stepped toward it before another loud bang shook the building. The spell broken, Garza pivoted toward the front of the building and barked something to his aides, and they all rushed away with great haste.

Kincaid pulled back and sighed as the door closed. He circled and jumped, startled.

Hanging a few feet in front of him were hundreds of Androids, their heads missing eyes, noses, teeth, the metal exoskeleton beneath exposed. Some were missing their bottom halves, others their top. Random legs, arms, and ribcages dotted the floor. Thin yellow IVs of synthetic blood ran throughout the entire room from the ceiling above, snaking like ivy into the more complete versions. Their eyes glimmered with half-life.

Some strange curiosity pulled him forward. Kincaid walked among the rows. He came to the end of one and there, crumbled on the floor, was the young boy from when Kincaid visited the Cluster before, yellow IVs snaking from his entire body. The boy's crumpled blond hair slightly askew from his exo-skull. The I LOVE NY t-shirt hung loosely on his frame.

Kincaid bent down and touched his face; his fingers met only the cold touch of metal.

He was an Android the entire time? So the entire thing was an act?

A clinking of metal interrupted his thoughts.

"Hello?" Kincaid called, stepping forward. The other Androids swayed, like chimes in the wind. As they parted, he saw a familiar face.

No, it can't be.

Kincaid ran through the rows, shoving the other Androids aside until he stood in front of it. Hanging from the ceiling like a discarded Pinocchio was an Android head and its metal spine with a familiar face. His face.

Kincaid's body went ice cold, his breath caught in the back of his throat. He recoiled back, his legs gave out, and he fell back into a row of Androids.

"*Bienvenido* home," a cool voice purred from behind him.

Kincaid turned and saw Mayor Garza standing at the end of the row, his hands neatly folded in front of him, his yellow eyes gleaming.

"All of your searching is now at an end," Garza continued, stepping toward Kincaid, his dark black shoes clapping against the metal floor loudly.

"Mayor Garza?" Kincaid choked, moving back, his mind swimming, spinning, black dots appearing at the edge of his vision.

Garza stopped in front of him and bent down, placing a hand on his shoulder. "Breathe," he said.

Kincaid closed his eyes. He inhaled. Exhaled. Inhaled again. The rhythm slowly calmed him. When he opened his eyes, Garza stood above him, offering his hand.

Kincaid declined, pushing himself off the floor shakily.

Garza nodded and turned, beckoning him to follow. "I'm sure you have many questions, *hijo*."

Kincaid's mind swirled with emotions, before uncontrolled rage exploded out of him. "Yeah, why did you kill my wife and daughter, you bastard?" he roared.

Garza pivoted, looking at him out of the corner of his yellow eye, like an apex predator brushing off a lesser.

"So you've recovered some memories, excellent. That means the last piece is *finally* within reach. As I said before, all of your searching has come to an end. You've been on a long journey, but soon you can rest easy, all your questions answered. Why did we kill your wife and daughter? The answer to that is simple: we didn't."

"What?" Kincaid whispered.

"Think about it, *hijo*. Why would we, HIVE, eliminate our only leverage over you?" Garza stated.

"Because you got what you wanted from me?" Kincaid challenged.

"That's where you're wrong. We never planned to let you go. Your knowledge proved to be invaluable to us. We knew if we let your wife and daughter go, you would turn that ferocious skill of yours back on us. Your wife and daughter were killed by none other than Alex Kyranos, himself," Garza answered.

What? That doesn't make any sense. I heard the voicemail...

"Confused?" Garza mocked, circling around him. "Alex was much more perceptive than you gave him credit for. He knew almost immediately when you started working for us. Like us, he knew we would never let you go. So he attempted to remove our leverage through a clandestine operation with his little club. Sadly, it went wrong, and your wife and daughter were the first of many casualties in his eventual quest for the code. He was wracked with guilt and tried desperately to stop you, to tell you the truth, but by the time he reached you, it was too late."

"Lies, he would've told me!" Kincaid shouted.

"That's the beautiful thing about a lie. You breathe it into the world and watch it grow, evolve. Before you know it, the lie you told looks completely different. In many ways, you were our greatest one. Come, I'll show you," Garza retorted, smiling, walking deeper into the room.

"When you discovered your wife and child had been killed, you did turn against us. You attempted to undo everything. Our former leader took your efforts a bit *personally*. I had been waiting in the wings for a perfect moment to expand my influence, and your actions presented the perfect opportunity. I persuaded him to take another course; we decided to use you as a guinea pig for a new memory extraction technology. We put you into the precursor of the current rig and began the process. Imagine our surprise when we found out about the code."

"I thought I erased my memory of the code?" Kincaid argued.

"You did, but the intention remained. Your thoughts and actions were tinged with such passion, such desire. Over time, we were able to tease out whispers, fragments, keeping tabs on Alex and his club filled in the rest."

Garza took them down a set of metal steps. Large, hissing pipes surrounded them on either side. The air grew warmer. He stopped in front of a large metal tank, several pipes feeding into it. Painted in faded gold block letters on the bottom was 01. A tiny, narrow, closed window latch with an access panel rested at about head level. Garza walked over to the panel and swiped his badge. The panel flashed green, and a small holographic keypad flashed out. He typed a sequence of numbers, the panel flashing green again. The latch opened, hissing, steam pluming out. He pulled against the heavy door; yellow light spilled out over Kincaid.

Garza stood to the side, smirking. "Go on, look," he leered.

Kincaid walked over to the window and looked inside. At first, all he saw was yellow fluid, but as he grew acclimated to the light, he made out a figure floating in the middle of the tank. The figure materialized, it was a naked human male, its skin pale and blue. Its head was covered in a helmet, wires coiling out of it. Hundreds of tiny lights flashed within them. Pain flashed through Kincaid's mind as he stared at them. He steadied himself against the side of the tank. He heard Garza typing something into the access panel, each entry followed by a loud beep. Bubbles appeared around the helmet, and it unlatched from the man's neck. As it floated away, the man's face came into view.

Kincaid staggered back, more shocked than before. His head flared and he spun toward Garza. The face within the tank was his own.

"I... don't know what to believe," Kincaid uttered.

"Ah, belief, it's a funny thing. You start to examine it closely and poof! The entire thing falls apart. You get trapped in a loop that would fall even the greatest AI!" Garza said, gesturing to the tank. The light within glowing eerily. "Is that his brain and feelings in your body? Are the holes in your memories simply trauma? Did we download parts of him into you? If so, is that what makes you him? Or are you, you all by yourself? The questions, the questions. Soon you're paralyzed by it. Shivering in the corner like a scared monkey who saw his own reflection.

"The point is belief isn't always knowledge. Belief didn't get you here. Place you into this scenario. Knowledge did. Knowledge of something powerful, something if HIVE controls, we'll the control the entire world forever. Here's the truth: the memory extraction process took its toll on the man known as Dashiell Kincaid. He was near death, but just before his heart gave out, we experienced a breakthrough. We discovered if we kept him in a semi-cryogenic state, we could extract enough memories to create a workable clone. It took time, we had many failures along the way, but finally, in came you: a perfect blend of human and Android technology. The next evolution in humanity. A marvel. My wonderful *hijo*," Garza stated, his eyes shining with greed.

"So I really am a... clone," Kincaid whispered.

"Yes, a clone built solely to lead us to the Terminal Code at first. But as you grew and we saw the things you could do for us in SCAPE, you became so much *more*," Garza replied.

"I've never heard more bullshit in my entire life," a voice said.

Kincaid pivoted.

Alex walked down the stairs toward them.

Garza's face flushed. "Ah, Senior Kyranos. I was wondering when you were going to join our little fiesta. What a gift you have brought!" he exclaimed.

Alex's eyes narrowed.

"Oh, yes," Garza continued. "We know all about your efforts to find the other pieces of the code, your little organization, your attempts to find and contact Kincaid, your plan to distract us by setting off a smoke bomb in the middle of the Cluster square. Nothing is hidden from HIVE for long. I thought you would know that by now."

Alex reached into his jacket, pulled out a gun, and pointed it straight at Garza's head. "I didn't bring it for you. I brought it for us," he declared, looking over at Kincaid. "For him."

Garza chuckled. "Don't insult me with your fake loyalty. We both know your friend is floating in that tank. This Kincaid is only a convincing double, one who you were perfectly happy using to get the final piece of the code for yourself."

Alex held the gun higher and cocked the hammer back. "Yes, I used him; we *both* used him. A means to a very long end. I wanted to take the code from HIVE so badly. I wanted to prevent you from taking control of both SCAPE and the real world and exploiting the few who remain in it. But no more. It's time for him to decide."

"How noble of you," Garza purred, pressing one of his cuff-links. There was the sound of a metallic release.

Two Androids fell from the ceiling in front of Garza. Their half-finished eyes glowed blue. They advanced toward Kincaid and Alex silently.

Alex fired his gun at the closest one, the bullet sinking in, yellow blood falling from the wound. It continued moving forward, undeterred.

"Run!" Alex yelled.

They bolted up the stairs, Alex struggling to keep up. His breath came in large heaving gasps. More Androids fell from the ceiling behind them, joining their fellows. Alex fired over his shoulder; the bullet glanced off one of the IVs, spilling yellow blood on the floor.

"You have anything stronger than that?" Kincaid yelled.

Alex grimaced, dug into his pocket, and pulled out a softball-sized metallic disk.

"Is that a mini-EMP?" Kincaid gasped.

Alex nodded and pressed a button in the center. A circle of blue dot lights appeared, flashing once before disappearing to just a single one. A moment went by and another lit up. When the circle was complete, so too, was the charge. A charge strong enough to take out every Android in the room.

But what will that do to me? Kincaid hoped to not find out.

More and more Androids dropped around them like vultures. They all chased after them, the lights on the disc turning on painfully slow.

Another contingent dropped down to their right, causing them to turn to the left. Kincaid turned back and gulped when the groups merged together. They surged toward them like angels of death.

Alex threw the disc over his head, and it landed in the center of the floor. The Androids swarmed around it, oblivious. The last dot of the circle lit up and the dots turned green before a giant blue wave burst out of it. The wave instantly shut down every Android it touched, each falling to the floor with a thud. It spread through the rows of Androids and moved toward Kincaid. He could only watch in horror as it neared. As it passed through him, a spike of hot pain erupted in his skull, followed by darkness, then white light and the pungent tang of ammonia.

Alex shook him awake, pulling him to his feet. "C'mon!" he shouted, dragging him toward the door.

"What happened?" Kincaid asked.

"You passed out for a second after the wave, but I managed to rouse you," Alex said, shaking a vial of smelling salts.

They burst out of the door into the hall toward a door across the way that read: *ADMINISTRATIVE.*

Kincaid waved his badge in front of the access panel, it lit green, and the door slid open. He went through first as a shot rang out from behind. They both turned back to see Garza running toward them, a tiny smoking pistol in his hand. Alex ran through the door, waved it closed, then used the butt of the gun to break the panel.

They leaned against the wall for a moment, breathing heavily. Alex was drenched in sweat; his skin looked clammy and feverish.

They were in a white room, two shiny chrome rigs in the center. A scared-looking Asian woman hovered over a holographic keyboard, typing frantically under the watchful eye of a HIVE employee who held a large gun threateningly. The employee noticed them and moved to grab his gun, but Alex shot first. Blood bloomed from the man's chest.

The woman shrieked and tried running toward the door when Alex raised the gun toward her.

She stopped, holding up her hands, her mouth open as she stared at the corpse.

"Strap us into these rigs now," Alex demanded.

The woman nervously nodded, returning to the keyboard, and typed in a sequence. The rigs hummed to life and opened like flower petals at dawn.

Alex gestured for Kincaid to get into the first and paled. He grabbed his side, now bloody.

"Alex, you got hit?" Kincaid said, coming over to him, concerned.

"Yea, Garza's a lucky fucker," Alex gasped, blood spreading. He shoved Kincaid off and motioned again for him to get into the rig.

Kincaid reluctantly laid down. The rig's seat oddly warm as if it was expecting him.

Alex turned to the woman. "Make sure we're right at the update point, nowhere else."

She nodded, typing, the arms of the rig descending over Kincaid. The faint buzz of static spread over his body as it warmed up, already linking his senses.

Alex staggered over, his bloodstain larger. He placed his hand over Kincaid's. "Don't worry," he gasped, gritting his teeth. "I'll see you in there, promise."

Kincaid was about to reply when electricity shot through his body and pulled him downward into SCAPE.

~~~

CHAPTER 18

Kincaid tumbled through the Abyss like a comet.

Streams of data flew by. He fell faster and faster until the Trinity Node appeared below him. Normally, he would streak toward one of its petals loading into a destination, but this time, he rocketed toward the center and, to his surprise, fell right through it as if it was water. Down and down he fell, the world growing deeper and darker.

How long he fell, he couldn't tell. Eventually, the air seemed to get thicker, as if he passed through some invisible barrier. Once through, his perspective shifted, and he went from falling down to falling up. A tiny speck of light rapidly approached from above. Soon, it overtook him, blinding him.

The light cleared.

Kincaid was lying—no, floating—on his back. A soft aquamarine light surrounded him. He sat up and was amazed. He was in the shallows of a massive data lake. Silver and gold streams of code shifted just beneath the surface. The streams flowed toward the center of the lake, where the data lifted up into the sky, forming a giant funnel like a supermassive black hole. The funnel stretched endlessly into a blue then deep black sky. Kincaid lifted his head and saw twinkles of that same data, sparkling like stars high above. Movement in his peripheral vision drew his attention.

Blank-faced, blocky utility Avatars swarmed around a half-completed wooden boat constructed of data. They flew up and down a polished metal dock that reflected the sky above and created a sharp contrast with the lake below. They hauled large square blocks of data toward the ship. Once they got close to it, the blocks shimmered, broke apart, and streamed toward it in individual bits, reassembling effortlessly into pieces of the vessel. A large data rope ran from it to a column at the end of the dock, and a large holographic timer floated just over the knot reading:

Time to Update Release: 00:10:00

"Beautiful, isn't it?"

Kincaid turned.

Alex stood in the shallows, wearing his Dick Tracy Avatar. He coughed, and the edges of the Avatar blurred, his bio-data alternating between gold and red.

Kincaid's brow furrowed. "You alright?"

Alex nodded and reached into his jacket, pulling out a tiny flask. He unscrewed the cap and took a deep pull, the smell of whiskey wafting. He shook his head afterward, gritting his teeth. He noticed Kincaid staring at him and smirked.

"Did you know you originally altered the base code of my Avatar to automatically convert a rig's hydration fluid to alcohol? Only a flask-full, of course; any more would be dangerous. Perks of the relationship, I suppose." Alex chuckled before his bio-data flared red again. "Let's hurry, we don't have much time," he said, walking toward the dock.

As they approached, the utility Avatars carried on, oblivious to their presence. That changed the instant Alex stepped onto it. All of the Avatars stopped, and the five closest to the edge turned toward them. Their faces and forms shifted, and they grew into large blocky naval security guards, wielding long, sparking electric tasers. They came closer, fast.

Kincaid held out his hand and exhaled.

The air around the guards flickered and materialized into rubber cages. The guards grew, trying to break free, but the cages stretched then shrank, pulling them down to their normal sizes. They banged their tasers against the walls but the rubber rendered the electricity useless.

"Nice," Alex chirped, walking fully onto the dock.

The other Avatars remained still, as if looking at their five fellows and shrugging, then resumed their duties around them.

Alex stopped at the end of the dock, looking up at the ship. Kincaid walked over and stood next to him. Alex reached into his jacket and pulled out the crystal vial; the dark smokey liquid of the terminal code floated within. He reached toward the stopper.

"Wait," Kincaid said. Alex paused, his fingers just above the stopper. "I need to ask you something first," he demanded.

Alex raised an eyebrow.

"Why...?" Kincaid said, looking out over the water. "Why did you change your mind?"

"What do you mean?" Alex asked.

"Before, in the mall, you seemed so determined, so willing to do anything to get the final piece. Then, in front of Garza and even now, you seem so at peace."

Alex chuckled. "I guess I do, don't I? Amazing how things change with perspective. Once I saw my friend in the tank, what they did to him, what they did to you, what they're *still* doing to you, I realized... if anyone has the right to decide what to do with this code, to decide the future of SCAPE, HIVE, both worlds, it was you. I only wish..." A single tear fell down his cheek, his bio-data turning a melancholic blue.

"I think I understand now," Kincaid said, placing his hand on Alex's shoulder and squeezing.

Alex sniffled and uncorked the vial. The violet code flooded out and merged into the ship, it grew in size, and a long mast sprouted out of the center. Alex turned toward Kincaid, waiting.

Kincaid didn't know how to get the final piece of the code into the update but he had to try. He inhaled, closed his eyes, and cleared his mind. Mysteriously, his hand floated up to his temple and pressed down. Something within him came *alive*, a twisting, burning thing. It coiled, scared to let go. Then, as if pulled by a giant magnet, it flew out of him. Kincaid opened his eyes.

A gold thread furled out of his torso and twisted toward the mast. The thread weaved around it and then grew. Spreading, knitting, fusing. The code swirled, and a great light grew within. It spread and enveloped the entire dock and when it faded, a glimmering golden sail hung over the mast, a red sun emblazoned in the middle. The sail flapped as if eagerly expecting a great wind to take it into the center of the lake and into all of SCAPE and beyond.

Thwack. One of the threads in the rope snapped. The clock now read:

Time to Update Release: 00:05:00

"How kind of you to put it together for me," a voice said from above.

The world went white and sideways, tinged in fire and pain. Kincaid and Alex flew through the air and tumbled right into the middle of the lake. They sunk for a moment. Kincaid grabbed Alex, cleared his mind, and they shot out of the water and hovered in the air.

Over the dock floated a new Avatar. He rotated toward them and grinned familiarly.

"Garza," Kincaid seethed.

Garza's Avatar's features were angular and cat-like, his eyes just like a lions but instead, glowed a fiery red. He wore a fitted black suit trimmed in black and gold with a HIVE logo stitched over his breast pocket. A red flower rested above. Blood-red bio-data curled throughout his form. He spread his fingers, and angry fire bloomed within. He grinned and hurled a fireball toward the ship. It exploded into flame.

"No!" Alex yelled.

They shot to the dock, and Alex and he dropped down in front of the burning vessel. The utility Avatars frantically scrambled around them, trying to put out the fire.

Garza waved his arm in a wide arc, and fireballs plumed out and struck each and every utility Avatar. They burst into flames and disappeared into bits.

Kincaid stood in front of the ship and visualized the flames dissipating. He closed his eyes. A wave of heat struck his face. Opening them, the flames were brighter and higher than before.

"We learned so much from you, *hijo*. First, it was the code. Then it was the realization that here in SCAPE, anything is possible. We can literally be Gods!" Garza roared from above him.

Kincaid turned toward the data lake and pulled on it with his mind. A small wave formed and headed toward the dock.

The wave raised up and was about to crest when another wave broadsided it. They collided and burst into data and foam.

"Problem is, once you know about it, countering is as easy as a thought," Garza said.

"Alex, you try to get that rope loose and send the update to the funnel!" Kincaid yelled.

Alex nodded.

Kincaid rose from the dock to Garza's height. They circled around each other like boxers. Fireballs bloomed between each of Garza's fingers. Kincaid cleared his mind, the air blurred, and his mage staff appeared, lightning crackling around the tip.

Garza flung his arms and fireballs flew toward Kincaid. He flicked his staff; lightning arced and branched out, meeting each of them in a giant explosion.

Meanwhile, Alex pulled at the rope, trying to fray it loose but it remained unmoved. "It's not working!" he yelled.

Kincaid dodged another fireball. He flung a lightning bolt toward Garza and pivoted toward Alex.

"You have to believe," he yelled.

Alex furrowed his brow and raised his hands over his head. The air shimmered, and his sword appeared. He swung down.

The rope snapped in two.

"Yes!" Alex exclaimed. He walked to the edge of the dock, put his hands against the boat, and pushed. It stood still, the code within dark. "I can't move it!" he yelled.

Kincaid ducked as a fireball flew overhead, singing the tips of his hair. He flung his staff, sending lightning toward Garza. The bolt just missed his face. They continued sending volleys back and forth.

Kincaid was never going to win like this. He glanced over at the clock, it read:

The flames grew higher, and the boat groaned, split, and fell into the water, disintegrating into bits. Garza laughed maniacally.

Kincaid cursed. Without the update as a vehicle, the code couldn't spread throughout SCAPE. He also didn't know how much damage Garza's flames might have done. As he searched his memory, he realized he had no idea how to fix it or even where to begin. That knowledge lay floating in a tank, a world away.

Garza's laughter continued as thick black smoke began to plume from the wreckage.

A shrill cry rang out above them both, drawing their attention. A star above twinkled then began falling toward them fast. It streaked down and landed in the middle of the data lake, sending waves outward like a Tsunami. When they settled, Kincaid made out the shape of a familiar tangerine box.

The box bowed before bursting open. Corpses of large cats flew out and crashed into the shallows, their bodies covered in deep lacerations. Emerging from the deep darkness of the box was a tall thin man wearing blood-covered surgical scrubs, a mask and goggles covering his face. One of his hands clutched a shining bone saw, the other a tiny but deadly-looking scalpel.

The man bent over one of the cats' corpses and kicked it, seeing if there was still life within. Satisfied, he dropped the bone saw and scalpel into the water and turned toward Garza and Kincaid. He reached up and removed his headgear, revealing familiar sparkling blue eyes.

"Told you I could take these pussies," Snoops gleefully declared.

"Snoops?" Kincaid gasped.

Snoops winked and bent down in a mock bow.

Kincaid couldn't believe it. AIs *never* got out of Schrodinger loops. Doing so was impossible, or at least so he thought. Garza's laughter, which had stopped momentarily, began again, this time louder than before. "*Finally!*" he shouted with glee as he floated down toward Snoops.

Snoops cocked his head, eyeing Garza up. "You don't look so tough," he stated.

Garza ignored Snoops as the black smoke from the boat plumed behind him. "At first, our plan was to destroy the code. But as we watched you, *hijo*, we made an even more startling discovery. Your AI here represents an anomaly. Something not bound by the rules of SCAPE. After observing and testing you both, we decided to make an alteration to the code. An alteration hidden in those fireballs I threw."

The smoke curled around Garza and shot straight into Snoops. Snoops lifted up and shifted, shining blue. The smoke turned red and integrated into the blue, turning it purple. Snoops floated back down to the water. He turned toward Kincaid, and the blank look in his eyes sent a chill through Kincaid's spine.

"What have you done?" he whispered.

"Simple. Achieve our goal. You and poor Alex here," Garza purred, "you never understood our true objective. We altered the code to take control of your AI here. It can interface with any machine in the real world, allowing us to execute our grand plan: we take control of every Android, drone, and HIVE bot in the world and use it to eliminate HIVE's pesky pockets of resistance all at once. Of course, after such a tragedy, the world will rightly demand answers. In their search, they'll come to a discovery: the latest SCAPE update contained a glitch. The public outrage will be swift and in the chaos, we will emerge with a solution. In the best interest of the public, HIVE will take control of SCAPE once and for all. With our real-world opposition gone, there'll be few roadblocks and if any make noise in SCAPE, well, we'll use the code's original purpose to silence them once and for all."

Kincaid gaped at Garza. His mind echoed with Hiroshi's warning, *someday they'll come for it.* "You're insane," he gasped.

Garza stared at him. "No, not insane. I'm simply a product of my environment. I grew up with *nothing.* My family and I were *basura* trash; we had to scratch and claw our way just to get the scraps. Constantly at the beck and call of more powerful sicarios, cartels, it didn't matter. I swore to myself I would never be like that again. Instead, I'd be like them. I'd be the one in control, the one who determines who lives and dies, the one with real power. Power like this."

Garza snapped his fingers. Snoops' head snapped toward him, and he walked quickly over to Garza and fell down to one knee asking, "What's your command, master?"

Garza's shoulders relaxed as if a great weight had been lifted, and he grinned even wider than before, the corners of his mouth stretching to cat-like proportions. "Snoops, why don't you show our friends here a demonstration of your new power? You can start with the rabble in New York City."

"Affirmative," Snoops replied coldly as he floated out over the lake and searched the waves before shooting down and plunging his hand into the water, firmly grasping one particular data stream. A violet light burst out of Snoops' hand into it and shot rapidly up into the funnel above.

Above Snoops, a large holographic screen appeared, its picture showing the skyline of New York City.

~~~

CHAPTER 19

Back in the real world, Victoria Wong was on crowd control. She and her unit stood in front of electric barricades that blocked the center of the Cluster from the alleys of Old Downtown. Every time SCAPE released an update, thousands of the city's homeless and other vengeful and forgotten souls marched on the Cluster in protest. They demanded HIVE, SCAPE, the city, and the world listen to their problems, their needs. Their desperation made violence just a stone's throw away.

Large HIVE security bots lurked just behind her unit, their guns gleaming darkly. Overhead, hundreds of police and media drones swarmed, watching, waiting.

Wong cursed.

She always hated her department being dragged into this monthly shit show. But as one of the few departments with human staff, she often got pulled into things like this for political reasons. Despite a world mostly enamored with SCAPE, an all-robot police force would conjure fear.

Behind her, as if oblivious to chaos, was the Portal. Its lighthouse beacon shone over the square with reckless abandon. The timer over it read:

The crowd pushed up against the barrier. The static crackled like a bullwhip against a restless herd. Victoria nervously raised her shotgun, gripping the barrel tighter. Random shouts and cursed swelled across the masses, hitting her ears.

"Fuck HIVE!!!"

"We're hungry. Why doesn't anyone feed us?"

"Why won't you help us, Mayor Garza?"

"Does anyone really care about the world anymore?"

As the shouting continued, Wong couldn't help but ask the same questions herself.

The crowd's voices swelled, raising to an almost violent crescendo when something suddenly hushed them. Wong looked toward the crowd, searching for the answer, when she noticed they were all staring at something behind her. She turned and her mouth dropped.

The Portal was *flickering*, briefly revealing the panels underneath. The Portal *never* flickered. As the main hub for SCAPE worldwide, it had its own dedicated power grid and numerous back-up systems. Then just as suddenly as it had begun, the flickering stopped. The lighthouse was restored, only this time, its beacon's light was bright violet.

Meanwhile, far beyond the Cluster in the city beyond, hundreds of users entered into their rigs, eager to join their friends and family at one of the many update celebrations held around SCAPE. As the rigs closed, their screens froze for a moment before a message displayed:

As part of a special update promotion, you've been selected to participate in a new exclusive beta game. The game will be live-streamed across SCAPE with

the winner collecting a special grand prize. Would you like to participate?

Y/N?

The users hungry for glory, money, and fame selected Y. Their screens went blank before their Avatars materialized into the cockpit of a hovercraft, their radars showing hundreds of red targets below. They eagerly grabbed the controls and moved the craft toward the targets.

Back in the Cluster, the HIVE bots and drones hovered, bathing in the violet light of the beacon. Their front screens faded for a moment before being replaced slowly with a violet HIVE symbol. They raised silently in unison.

In SCAPE, the users angled their crafts closer to their targets. The red dots resolved into grotesque alien monsters who spewed venom and shot lasers toward the crafts. The users angled up their sights and pulled the triggers.

The HIVE bots and drones swarmed and opened fire on the crowd below. Bodies disappeared in clouds of blood and smoke.

Wong looked on in horror as the drones tore the crowd into pieces. Those not killed in the initial pass ran screaming into the alleys of Old Downtown as if the twists and turns could somehow save them. The drones and HIVE bots followed like a metallic death squad. Wong turned to her unit, her men's faces ghost white with shock.

What the fuck is going on? she thought before ordering her men after the robots.

~

The screams of the crowd echoed from the screen across the data lake, chilling Alex and Kincaid's hearts.

Garza drank the scene in with rapt attention, his eyes gleaming as red as his blood lust. Kincaid clenched his staff and, with a bellow, shot a bolt of lightning straight into Garza. The bolt struck, lifting Garza into the air and flinging him into the middle of the lake. He burst from the water, his eyes dripping with malice.

He turned to Snoops and demanded, "Snoops, remove this annoyance from my sight."

Snoops turned slowly toward Garza and replied, "Master, if I stop the transmission now, I estimate only a 40 percent completion of your primary objective. Your code's directive was clear: do not stop until 100 percent of dissidents are eliminated."

"I don't care about the directive. Eliminate them now!" Garza hissed.

Alex came over to Kincaid slowly and raised his sword. "I'll take Snoops; you take Garza," he said, panting heavily.

Kincaid eyed Alex skeptically, but Alex cut the argument short by swinging his sword and sending a green energy crescent toward Snoops.

The crescent was inches from Snoops when he held out his index finger. The crescent dissolved in a flash of light. He raised his hand toward Alex. Alex's Avatar shimmered, his bio-data flaring as he fell to a knee then face down into the ground, dropping his sword into the lake.

"Half of your threat level has been eliminated, Master. I will now return to my primary directive," Snoops reported.

Garza was about to reply when the screams began to lessen on the screen. The HIVE bots and drones were slowing down. Garza looked from them to Kincaid and grit his teeth. "Fine, return to your directive. I'll eliminate this one myself."

Snoops nodded.

Kincaid wasted no time and shot a bolt straight at Garza's head. Garza flicked his wrist and sent a fireball into the water, creating a burst of steam as he dodged.

Kincaid clenched his jaw. Fighting like this was pointless. Even if he somehow beat Garza here, he still had to deal with Snoops, not to mention nothing would stop Garza from finding his body in the real world and slowly prying it from the rig. He needed to stop both of them here and now.

As Kincaid pondered, *something* brushed his mind. He examined it and was amazed. It was a piece of the code, still somehow attached to him. He reached out toward it, and it responded quickly, glowing with expectation. He smiled; he had a plan.

Kincaid moved his hand to the middle of his staff and spun it. Black smoke shot out of both ends and covered him completely.

Garza paused. "Hiding now? You must be desperate, not that it matters much anyways."

Garza slammed his hands together and pulled them slowly apart, a large fireball sprouting between them. He raised his arms over his head and spread them out, the fireball growing in size as he did. Soon his entire body was bathed in the red glow of the massive sun above him. He grunted and flung the fireball toward the smokescreen.

Garza laughed as the fireball reached the smoke and passed through, flying down into the data lake and exploding with a massive burst. As it cleared, Garza flew lower, looking for signs of Kincaid's Avatar.

Thunder rumbled overhead.

Garza lifted his head and saw Kincaid high above, his entire body crackling with lightning. He held his staff toward the sky, a large storm cloud swirling above, blue lightning flashing from within. Kincaid lowered the staff, and a huge bolt erupted from the cloud, arching straight into Garza's chest, flinging him violently into the lake right next to Snoops.

The water sung with charge from the blast. Kincaid breathed heavily as he searched the surface, waiting. Watching. As bubbles trickled from the depths right next to an unfazed Snoops, Kincaid steeled himself. Soon Garza would surface.

The surface rumbled. This was the moment. He called on the code.

Hold them.

Garza emerged from the lake. He leered at Kincaid and was ready to leap into the air, when a golden thread materialized and wrapped itself around Snoops and him.

Garza chuckled and pulled against it as the thread multiplied, shooting around his and Snoops' arms, waist, and neck. The threads pulled him down to one knee.

Snoops sat entrapped, his hand clutching the data stream, his focus unperturbed.

"Another silly trick, pathetic," Garza mocked.

Kincaid shook his head. "No, this is also part of the code. I put you between it and its other half. It desperately wants to be complete."

"What?" Garza mocked as the threads tightened, pulling Garza and Snoops closer.

"Let me ask you a question, Garza," Kincaid stated. "You may have altered the Terminal Code, but at its core, it's still a code designed to do one thing: destroy. What do you think will happen when it infects you?"

Garza's laughter weakened, and his face paled as it dawn on him. His bio-data screamed in protest.

The threads continued inching closer together. Garza began to frantically squirm, pulling against the threads, firing fireballs into it, screaming for Snoops to intervene. Nothing worked. As Kincaid watched, he felt a strange emotion: pity. Did Garza deserve to die?

Kincaid could easily use the code as a distraction, take Alex, and run away, giving them the opportunity to regroup, marshal their forces, and live to fight another day. Not to mention, Garza could still mercilessly hunt them down in both worlds. On the other hand, Garza's death would deal a serious blow to HIVE. He was the center of political life in the city. If he were removed, HIVE would be stunned and need time to recover.

Kincaid's mind shifted to the terrible things he'd done to Emily and Rose. The terrible things he'd done to *both* of him. The masses he deluded, the people he was killing now and would kill in the future. He gritted his teeth, his mind made up. Garza could not continue.

Integrate.

The thread began constricting faster.

"No! You wouldn't *dare!* Without me, you'll never stop your AI. You may stop me, but another will rise to take my control of it and soon the world. HIVE has many masters," Garza yelled, his voice defiant but his eyes glowing with panic.

The thread stopped. Garza's eyes lit up with hope before they snapped together, pulling Garza's Avatar straight into Snoops. When they collided, the violet code burst from Snoops straight into Garza. His eyes widened as his Avatar shook, large blue cracks spreading over his entire body. His bio-data lit up and lifted up over his Avatar, forming a miniature funnel, just like the one above the lake. Garza's body was pulled back as if something was being ripped from within by a cruel puppet master. He let out a deep guttural yell as his Avatar burst, the data flowing through the funnel followed by the code.

In the real world, Garza's rig nodes flashed purple. Lightning shot out of the ends of the nodes straight into his heart, shaking his entire body furiously before stopping. Smoke curled from his now burnt flesh. Blood dripped from the corner of his mouth. His yellow eyes were open in shock, their brilliance now reduced to cloudy amber.

Back in SCAPE, the light faded, leaving Kincaid, Snoops, and Alex.

Kincaid looked at Snoops, waiting for a reaction, but he continued holding the data stream.

Kincaid floated down to the dock toward Alex's Avatar. If the damage was severe enough, his Avatar would auto-log out. The fact his was still here meant he was still some level away from the threshold. Kincaid bent down and shook Alex.

Alex was still for a moment before coughing. Green code slithered away from his center. He turned around to Kincaid. "Did you win?" he asked.

Kincaid smiled weakly. "Sorta," he replied.

Alex looked out over the lake and spotted Snoops and looked around for Garza. He lifted an eyebrow. Kincaid nodded.

"So you rid New York of that bastard!" Alex coughed.

"*We* got rid of him." Kincaid laughed, giving him a side-hug.

Alex smiled weakly then coughed again. His bio-data flared. His Avatar blurred and disappeared, leaving Kincaid alone with Snoops. The pain threshold had been reached.

Kincaid floated over to Snoops, landing softly behind him. He had no idea how to stop him. As he reached out his hand to touch Snoop's shoulder, the violet code within swirled, hungry for its next victim. He didn't even know if the code would let him touch Snoops or instead tear him into bits, joining him with his original permanently. But he knew one thing—he had to try and protect SCAPE.

He reached out, the code swarmed, and he was swallowed.

~~~

CHAPTER 20

———

Kincaid's consciousness floated, and he began to perceive shapes, forms, slowly resolving into twinkling blue bits circling in cosmic symmetry.

The bits swirled, coming closer together. They formed into a small sphere, a deep blue glowing from the center. A little girl's dark silhouette appeared before the light flashed and faded, revealing soft auburn curls.

"Rose?" Kincaid whispered, his heart suddenly filled with immense love and joy.

The little girl stepped closer, exposing her bright blue eyes.

"Hiya, boss," the girl said.

"Snoops? How!" he gasped.

She grinned. "It's a long story, but you can call me back-up Snoops."

"What do you mean?"

"You, er, the *other* you figured this might happen. So he made a back-up of me and placed me in the last piece of code with a program that would trigger under certain conditions."

Kincaid was shocked. He couldn't believe his predecessor had such forethought. It was prescience bordering on—

"Impossible?" Snoops replied, cocking her head. "Didn't you learn *anything* from all this? You need to believe in yourself. Though I *may* have helped a tiny bit."

Did she—?

"Read your mind? Duh. I've been in your head this entire time, dummy!" she reprimanded, her hands on her hips.

Kincaid shook his head.

"Now you must choose," a familiar voice said.

Suddenly, they were inside of Kincaid's parents' living room. The TV sat across from the couch, and an old N64 console sat on the floor.

Hiroshi Takahashi strode into view, his hair pure white, eyes twinkling.

"Hiroshi?" Kincaid exclaimed.

Hiroshi walked past him and stood next to Snoops, placing his hand on her shoulder.

"I don't understand, what do you mean, choose?" Kincaid asked, his mind swimming, his memory distant and foggy.

Hiroshi chuckled. "You didn't just copy Snoops. Within her is the true version of the Terminal Code. The one ramping havoc now is just a dummy version, albeit a very convincing one. Your choice is simple: the code or Snoops."

Kincaid gasped, looking between Snoops and Hiroshi, waiting for one of them to grin, revealing a cruel joke. But neither did.

"Before you decide, let me tell you a story." Hiroshi sighed, walking forward, the room shifting to a pale version of the rooftop garden from years ago.

Kincaid followed, Snoops skipping behind them.

"When you began developing the Terminal Code, your first thought was to turn over the administration and execution of the code completely to AI. But your fear was that very AI could be taken over or corrupted by some external party. You pondered for months for a solution. Eventually, you decided to build a robust monitor AI system, able to contain any AI within SCAPE."

"The Schrodinger system," Kincaid breathed.

Hiroshi nodded. "You called it the perfect fusion of order and protection. But when you were about to launch the program, you discovered something in the base layer of the code. Something incredible. An emergent personality within the program. A natural born AI."

Snoops giggled.

"As you examined it, you became more amazed. The AI's personality was akin to a child, wanting desperately to watch, explore, and experience everything. Like a parent, you became protective, possessive. Soon, you began to doubt your original plan. You couldn't bring yourself to pollute such a being with the burden of the code. So you hedged. You split the program into two, hiding one portion of the code within the Schrodinger system and the other within Snoops. You used the time to go on adventures with Snoops, exploring SCAPE and beyond. But eventually..."

"HIVE," Kincaid hissed.

"You came to me right after," Snoops interrupted. "You knew if they captured you, they would find the code and eventually me. So you and I created the dummy version. Then you ordered me into your real-world implant and went and hid it around SCAPE. When you finished, you used part of it on yourself, wiping away most of your memories."

"Something doesn't add up," Kincaid stated, turning to Hiroshi. "If the code out there was a dummy the whole time, why have people died?"

"The codes are almost identical. The primary difference between the two is their range. The dummy only works in a ten-mile radius. Had either Alex or HIVE tried to use it outside of that range, it would've failed," Hiroshi stated.

"I forgot to mention!" Snoops exclaimed. "You gave me one final task. You asked me to hide in SCAPE, guarding a program you wrote until it activated. So I did. I hid for years and man was it boring! I was about to lose my mind when 'Ping!' your program lit up!"

"What did this program do?" Kincaid asked.

"It was a sniffer program that searched SCAPE for a unique piece of your bio-data. When it located you, I followed it and was shocked. There your Avatar was, warts and all. You were super lame and brainwashed at first. But I managed to undo that over time and insert the program into your Avatar's root code. The program that had a back-up version of me and the true version of the code. After that, we had tons and tons of adventures!" She grinned.

"What now?" Kincaid asked.

Hiroshi shrugged. "Beats me. I'm not real after all. I'm just something your brain made up to help contextualize everything!" Hiroshi laughed and vanished with a grin, the garden fading back to Kincaid's parents' living room.

Kincaid turned to Snoops. Her eyes were now serious.

"Option A," she said, holding up one hand, "you execute the code. I will merge with my original version. Its half of the code taken from the Schrodinger system will merge with mine. We will initiate a mass forced log out of everyone in SCAPE. They will not log back in until they accept new terms and conditions. These terms, if accepted, will dissolve SCAPE as a corporation, making the entire system and its code open-source. HIVE could change SCAPE, but so could everyone else; it'd be a true frontier. However, if less than 50 percent of the global user base declines the terms, a tapeworm program will activate, instantly destroying SCAPE."

"What will happen to you?" Kincaid asked.

"Based on my calculations, there's a 99.9 percent probability the fusion will reformat much of my root data and personality matrix, if the tapeworm doesn't get me first."

"So you'll die?" he whispered.

Snoops shrugged. "My data will remain, simply shuffled around in a new form. But in human terms, I suppose the answer is yes, I will die."

"What about option B?"

"Option B is you destroy the code. There's a self-destruct sequence you programmed into it. Something to do with a *Mortal Kombat combo*. You execute that, and I'll fuse together and both codes will terminate. But there's no guarantee I'll survive."

"What choice is that?" Kincaid yelled. His mind flooded with memories of his adventures with Snoops. Unlike the others he'd recently gained, these were vibrant, full of joy and, more importantly, they felt like *his*. Emotion bubbled.

"Snoops, I can't lose you." he uttered, fighting to choke back tears.

To his surprise, Snoops mimicked him. Her tears tinged with blue data. She shifted into an older version of herself, one that looked just like Emily, and came over, sitting him down on the couch before perching next to him.

"I'm just a virtual being," she stated. "Despite your strange circumstances, you are still human-*ish*, bound to the world in which you were born with a duty to your species. Am I worth the oppression of billions? Am I worth the destruction of your world? This is your choice; this was *always* your choice. Now make it."

An old N64 game cartridge on the table began to glow gold.

Kincaid looked over at Snoops.

"If you place that cartridge within the N64 and press start," she said solemnly, "you'll choose option A."

The controller next to it glowed silver.

"If you pick up that and enter the combo, you'll go with option B."

Kincaid bent down and picked up both. Each was heavier than it looked. He flipped the cartridge over in one hand and looked underneath; there were millions of lines of code within. He thought of the chaos the world would undergo if SCAPE were to disappear. The billions of lives forced to live again in the real world. The pain, the terror, the deaths. He remembered the beauty of SCAPE, the wonder and joy it brought to billions. Worlds of strange and exciting possibilities, many still unknown, waiting to be discovered.

Kincaid snapped out of his daze and realized he had risen from the sofa and hovered directly in front of the console.

Snoops gently rose from the couch, came up in front of him, grabbed his hand, and looked deeply into his eyes. "I had so much fun with you," she declared, tears streaming down her face.

"I know, me too," he avowed.

Snoops squeezed his hand tightly.

Kincaid bent down to put the cartridge in the case. His hand floated over to the start button and was about to press down when a glimmer caught his eye.

It was an old metal picture frame. Inside was a photo of Alex, his parents, and him at an amusement park. It was one of those rare photos that perfectly captured a moment.

They all stood in front of an ice cream stand. Alex and Kincaid were both young, about six years old. A dog ran right into his father's leg as the camera flashed. His father fell into Alex, whose cone flew and went sideways into young Kincaid's face, his own falling out of his grasp. His mother had already been knocked over, her face covered in the remnants of her own ice cream, her cone planted firmly in-between her outstretched legs. Her bottom lip stuck out in a state of shock and the shadow of a pout just like Rose used to do.

Kincaid began to laugh deeply. He laughed so hard tears fell from the corner of his eyes. His sides hurt with the effort. Snoops looked at him, concerned.

Kincaid shook his head. Looking at the photo reminded him of something. Life was inherently and utterly messy. Despite his love for order, nothing can change that, not even technology.

Any technology used by humans would ultimately come to inhabit *some* of the flaws of humanity itself. As he looked at Snoops, he realized it could also capture some of its greatest strengths.

He lunged toward the controller, his fingers entering the combination. Snoops' eyes widened as the world faded to white.

~

In the real-world, Victoria Wong had just fired her last shotgun round.

The round bounced harmlessly off the hull of one of the military drones. It came closer, violet eye blazing.

She looked back at her men as it approached. Many of them were bloody and wounded, a few dead, and she searched their faces. All were exhausted; none had any ammo left. They had chased the drones and HIVE bots for nine blocks into Old Downtown, trying desperately to draw their attention and save at least some lives. Their efforts were futile. Hundreds, if not thousands, had died.

Now the reaper had come from them too.

The violet light of the drone swept over them as its rail guns lowered. Wong and her men waited for the click, but the light vanished and the drone crashed violently to the street, its screen blank.

Wong and her men looked at each other in shock, then ahead as the other drones and HIVE bots fell to the earth, their faces also blank. The few survivors from Old Downtown clustered around the bots, cautiously waiting, ready to flee.

The crowd exhaled and began to cheer.

Wong smiled, and she looked at the mass of humanity around her begin to hug, kiss, and celebrate with one another. Wong looked at her men and felt her pride swell at what they had accomplished today with so few. She glanced back at the Cluster and had a feeling her unit was about to get a whole lot bigger.

~

Kincaid opened his eyes, and the stars of SCAPE greeted him.

He lifted himself off the ground and saw her.

Snoops lay face-up in the water, in her young girl form. Her colors were washed out and gray. Kincaid rushed over to her, pulling her out of the water and over to the dock. He gently placed her head onto the ground and whispered, "You still with me?"

Snoops laid still.

Kincaid closed his eyes and began to weep.

Her eyelids flickered. She stirred with a deep moan.

Kincaid's eyes sprung open. "Snoops!" he exclaimed.

Snoops slowly opened her eyes, her pupils now a soft lavender. "Hiya, boss, what...? What happened? I feel weird like I got smushed together or something. Is this what your hangovers feel like?" she asked, shaking her head.

Kincaid smiled and hugged her tightly. "I destroyed the code," he replied.

Snoops stared at him in disbelief, her eyes the size of dinner plates. "You destroyed the code! I can't believe it. What about SCAPE? What about HIVE?"

Kincaid smiled. "I realized something. SCAPE is loved by billions of people. That love means something. If they know it's being threatened by HIVE, they'll stand up to protect it. And they won't be doing it alone. As for HIVE, let's see what two back-ups can do!"

Snoops smiled, her entire body glowing with joy. They stood together on the dock and looked at the data floating up into the sky that shimmered with newfound hope.

~~~

THE END

ACKNOWLEDGMENTS

Wow.

It's hard to believe my first publishing journey has come to an end. Getting this book out into the world wouldn't have been possible without the hard work and dedication of many people. However, I'd be a terrible husband if I didn't first thank my beautiful wife, Jamie.

For those who don't know, I wrote most of this book while Jamie was pregnant with our first child. I also wrote it while working full-time and getting my MBA at Georgetown at night. To say Jamie has been patient with me throughout this entire process is a massive understatement. Jamie, thank you for letting me take a chance on my dream. It means the world to me, and I promise you'll have me back and ready to do house projects soon.

To my daughter, Amelia. Dada thanks you for coming into the world nineteen days after he submitted draft one and not learning how to smile and laugh until somewhere between drafts two and three and, of course, for being you. Amazing, wonderful, you.

Next, I'd like to thank my parents, sister, grandparents, aunts, uncles, and my cousins for being encouraging, supportive, and not making *too much* fun of my word choices at the dinner table during family zoom calls and more.

I'd also like to thank my wife's family (particularly Dr. Amo) for helping to get the word out about the book and connecting me with working authors. It really all does come back to Mars.

To my friends; in lots of ways this book wouldn't be what it is without you either. Some of the dialogue and lines in this book are from the notes app in my phone. Snippets of inspiration captured during concerts, parties, dinners, hangouts, and more. Thank you for helping me capture some of the magic, and if you read closely, there might even be an inside joke or two!

Special thanks to my early beta readers, George and Rita. Your insights and feedback were very crucial in getting this book to where it is today.

Of course, none of this would have happened without the efforts of one Mr. Eric Koester. Professor Koester, as I know him, reached out to me on LinkedIn asking if I wanted to take a leap of faith and finally write that book. I'm so glad I said yes. Thank you to Professor Koester, Brian Bies, Michael Bailey, Mozelle Jordan, and the entire NDP team for being patient with me and my insane schedule. I think we can all be proud of this novel.

Special shout-out to the following artists/bands/musicians whose own art and work has helped make creating mine that much easier by providing late-night playlists, early-morning albums, and rainy weekend afternoon live sets. In no particular order: Khruangbin, Mat Zo, Daft Punk, Louis the Child, SG Lewis, DJ Complexion (Future Beats Radio), Griz, EARTHGANG, Kaytranada, Dua Lipa, Gorillaz, Arc De Soleil, Jungle, Lettuce, Phish, String Cheese Incident, Black Pumas, Leisure, Remi Wolf, and much more.

Last but not least, thank you to all those who supported the book during its Indiegogo campaign phase! Without your support, the book wouldn't have gotten to this point. Special thanks to:

Matthew S	Kevin C
Catie P	Austin P
Steve B	Jaclynn L
Patricia M	Justin M
Stephanie M	Richard J
Richard Be	Richard Br
Bryant N	Kevin F
Mike B	Jamie W
Susan S	Peter R
William M	Venkat N
Jesse E	Drew H
Lisa C	Ross P
Carl A	Patrick R
Greg Z	Mark B
Slater W	Marc W
Lauren A	Matt M
Sana A	Teresa M
Matthew B	Vin M
Mitch R	Samantha R

Alexandra D

Patrick B

Hunter S

Dana W

Ross S

Kyle H

Cara N

Malachi K

Alicia C

Alec J

Michael & Leslie B.

Garry G

Cynthia B

Russell H

Steve M

Josh T

OJ C

Michelle H

William K

Julian V

Jay C

Roslyn E

Tucker R

Ashley H

Erica G

Debora A

Jameson R

George C

Bailey M

Cameron B

Bryan & Kayla L

Thuy S

Sheryll A

Keith A

Will H

Rob M

Mohammed D

Britton T

Amanda P

Jessica P

Brandon N

Jessica Y

Chris R

Gregg V

Jeanne G

Karen C

Debbie G

Dana V

Barbara H

Joyce b

Dominic R

Kevin T

Morgan D

Tracy P

Umi K

Jason V

Diego R

Julie I

Dawn M

Justin F

Eric K

Tony V

Morgan V

Jessica V

Heidi G

Brandon F

Rick N

Kaitlynn V

Italia P

Amy W

James B

Tierney M

Sharon M

Jennie H

Melanie L

Damian W

Chris D

Danya S

Alex B

Linda S

Elise K

Paul M

Rey P

J.W. Galliger
August 2021

APPENDIX

AUTHOR'S NOTE

Huxley, Aldous. *Ends and Means.* NY/London: Harper and Brothers Publishers, 1937.